The Book On

I0458839

Artificial Leverage

How to Use Tools, Technology, and Systems to Outwork Entire Teams Without Burnout

The Book On Series #14

David Webb

Published by The Book On Publishing, 2025.
First edition. July 26, 2025.

Website, https,//thebookon.ca
Substack, https,//thebookonpublishing.substack.com/

Artificial Leverage, How to Use Tools, Technology, and Systems to Outwork Entire Teams Without Burnout

First edition. July 26, 2025.

Copyright © 2025 The Book On Publishing

ISBN, 978-1-997795-72-8

Written by David Webb

Other Books In The Book On Series

Read This First

This is not a book designed to entertain you. It's not here to charm, to soothe, or to hold your hand. It won't dazzle you with stories, metaphors, or motivational fluff. What you're having is a tool, an instruction manual written for people who are serious about learning, executing, and thinking at a higher level.

Every book in The Book On Series is built on a single premise, clarity beats complexity. We believe that when you strip away the noise, the emotions, the marketing spin, and the cultural rituals of "self-help," what's left is raw, unembellished instruction. That's what these books offer.

They are dry by design. Not because we don't care about language or narrative, but because when you're building something that matters, you don't need more distractions. You need a clear architecture. Mental scaffolding. Direction that respects your intelligence.

Each title in this series takes on a specific domain, decision-making, clarity, strategy, leverage, and uncertainty, and drills deep, not in sweeping generalizations, but in applied frameworks. These are books for builders, operators, founders, tacticians, and thinkers—people who don't just consume knowledge but operationalize it.

You'll find no chapter-long anecdotes here. No self-congratulatory memoirs. No bullet-point platitudes. Instead, what you'll get is structured insight, argument, example, application. The tone is direct. The prose is sober. The ideas are designed to be lifted out and used.

You won't be coddled, but you won't be misled either.

There's a place in the world for lyrical, emotional, story-driven books, and this isn't that place. This is a workspace. A blueprint. A conversation for people who are ready to act, not just absorb.

We respect your time and your intellect.

Welcome to The Book On Series.

Table of Contents

Dedication

To the builders who never stopped asking,
"Is there a better way?"

To the solopreneurs, creators, and thinkers
Who chose design over hustle,
clarity over chaos,
And systems over sacrifice.

This book is for you—
Not because you wanted to do it all,
But because you dared to believe
You shouldn't have to.

—David Webb

Acknowledgments

This book could not have existed without the countless creators, founders, solopreneurs, and systems thinkers who unknowingly shaped its philosophy through the way they work, build, and rethink what's possible.

To the early adopters of automation who took the time to share what broke, and more importantly, what didn't. To the software engineers who made it possible for ideas to scale without human hands. To the creatives who proved that constraint breeds innovation. And to the readers of this series, who have come to expect books that challenge the way things are done, your support makes it worth writing them.

A special thanks to those in my circle who live this leverage life without fanfare. You taught me that intelligence isn't about doing more but about designing smarter. That margin isn't laziness, it's wisdom. That freedom isn't earned by burnout—it's engineered through clarity.

This book is built on your shoulders.

Thank you for thinking long, building well, and sharing generously.

—David Webb

Prologue

Why leverage, not effort, is the new power source for modern work

There's a quiet revolution happening.

You won't see it in boardrooms or corporate press releases. You'll see it in coffee shops and home offices, in small studios and remote work setups. You'll see it in creators, coders, consultants, and entrepreneurs who seem to produce like a team of ten, without actually hiring one.

They aren't superhuman. They're not burning out. And they aren't doing more in the traditional sense. What they've done is built something invisible but powerful. Something that allows them to operate at a level once reserved for companies with payrolls, managers, and quarterly meetings.

They've built *leverage* through tools, technology, and systems.

We've spent decades being told that the key to success was to work harder, work longer, and stay disciplined. And for a long time, that worked. But something fundamental has shifted. In today's economy, effort without architecture is like rowing a boat with one oar. You'll get tired long before you get anywhere.

We've crossed into a new era where the primary constraint on output is not effort, it's imagination. Not workforce, but system design. The modern advantage doesn't go to those who hustle the hardest. It goes to those who build systems that never sleep.

This book is for those who are ready to escape the myth of more effort. It's for the entrepreneurs and creatives who want to scale without exhaustion. It's for the thinkers, builders, and operators who understand that what matters most now isn't how much you can do, but how well you can build something that does it for you.

One Person, Infinite Output

The promise of technology wasn't just speed. It was scale.

What used to require an entire organization, a team of assistants, departments, and logistics, can now be run by a well-equipped individual. One person with the right tools can outpace entire companies.

But most people don't see this yet. They're stuck trying to compete with yesterday's playbook, work longer hours, hustle harder, take fewer breaks, read another book on grit.

That's not a strategy. That's a slow-motion collapse.

The fundamental shift is recognizing that output is no longer about the quantity of your labor. It's about the *quality of your leverage.* That includes how you structure your time, your workflows, your tech stack, your delegation systems, and your mental bandwidth.

Every repeatable task is an opportunity for automation. Every decision you make more than once is a candidate for codification.

Every piece of insight can be turned into an asset. Every interaction can be reimagined as a system.

What emerges is something powerful, *The Infrastructure of One.* A digital framework that supports your creativity, amplifies your productivity, and protects your sanity.

The Trap of Doing It All

Most talented people hit a ceiling.

It doesn't matter how skilled or motivated you are; eventually, you run out of hours. You reach a point where the to-do list grows faster than your ability to execute. You start working nights, then weekends. You sacrifice sleep, relationships, and focus to keep up.

That ceiling is where most people either stall or burn out. But it's also where a few people take a different path. They stop trying to do it all. And they start asking better questions,

> ➢ How can this run without me?
> ➢ What would this look like if it scaled automatically?
> ➢ Is this something I should even be doing at all?

That's where leverage begins. Not with a fancy tool or a flashy app, but with a mindset shift, from laborer to architect, from operator to orchestrator.

The Age of Artificial Leverage

We've always had forms of leverage, capital, labor, and influence. But now we have something new, artificial leverage.

Artificial leverage is the ability to use systems, software, and scalable tools to produce outcomes that vastly exceed the amount of effort you put in. It's what enables one person to schedule thousands of emails, manage dozens of client pipelines, launch content daily, and respond to customer requests without manual intervention.

This isn't hype. It's happening right now.

AI can write, summarize, transcribe, analyze, recommend, design, and forecast. Automation platforms can connect your tools, notify your team, update your records, and trigger events, all while you sleep. Low-code and no-code builders let you prototype ideas and deploy workflows without needing a developer.

And yet... most people are still doing everything the hard way.

They're sending emails manually, rewriting the same proposals, and managing their calendars by hand, all while wasting cognitive energy on tasks that should have been offloaded weeks ago.

The result? Overwhelm. Frustration. Burnout disguised as busyness.

But it doesn't have to be this way. You can reclaim your time. You can protect your focus. You can build systems that do the work, even better than you could do it yourself.

This Book Is a Blueprint

This book is not about theory. It's not about motivation. It's not about adding another thing to your already impossible list.

It's about subtraction through systems. Multiplication through infrastructure. Liberation through leverage.

In the chapters ahead, we'll break down exactly how to build an automated backbone for your business or solo career. You'll learn to think like a systems architect, not a task manager. You'll design processes that require less effort and deliver more consistency. You'll identify what to delegate, what to automate, and what to eliminate.

And most importantly, you'll learn to separate *your value* from *your labor.*

This is the power of artificial leverage. It's the invisible force that lets you scale without stretching. It's the missing piece for people who are already doing good work but need a more innovative way to keep up with the scale of modern demand.

So no, this is not a book about hustle. It's a book about building machines, machines that do the hustle for you.

You don't need to be superhuman. You need to build like someone who knows what's possible.

Welcome to the one-person revolution.

PART I — Foundations of Leverage Thinking

Chapter 1, Beyond Human Scale

When Marcus started his consulting practice, the simplicity was intoxicating. He answered emails himself, drafted proposals late into the evening, onboarded clients manually, and delivered every piece of work with careful attention. The effort felt pure. The growth felt earned. Each new client was proof that the long hours were working.

For a while, they were.

His revenue climbed steadily. Referrals increased. His reputation strengthened. Friends admired his discipline. From the outside, he looked like a textbook example of momentum. But something subtle was shifting beneath the surface, something he couldn't quite articulate at first. His calendar began to resemble a defensive formation rather than a design. Every day filled itself before he had the chance to think. His mornings started with email and ended with loose threads. The more successful he became, the less control he felt.

What unsettled him most was not the workload itself. It was the realization that every moving piece depended on him. If a proposal needed drafting, he drafted it. If a client needed onboarding, they initiated it. If a follow-up email had to be sent, it waited in his mind until he remembered. He had built something profitable, but it operated at the speed of his attention.

One evening, after rescheduling the same client twice because of overlapping obligations, Marcus found himself staring at his calendar with an unfamiliar question forming in his head, what would happen if I stopped working for a week?

He ran the thought experiment seriously. Leads would stall because he personally responded to inquiries. Proposals would sit unfinished. Invoices would go unsent. Deliverables would pause midstream. Nothing catastrophic would occur immediately, but everything would slow, and some things would quietly decay. The business was not fragile in terms of demand; it was fragile in terms of dependence.

That was the first time he recognized the ceiling he had hit. It wasn't a revenue ceiling. It wasn't a skill ceiling. It was a structural ceiling. No matter how efficient he became, there were only so many decisions he could make in a day, only so many hours he could concentrate deeply, only so many conversations he could manage before clarity deteriorated. His growth was tethered to the biological limits of one nervous system.

He began to examine his week with a different lens. Not by counting hours, but by observing patterns. He noticed how many tasks repeated predictably, onboarding emails that differed only slightly from the previous week's version, proposals structured in nearly identical formats, scheduling threads that followed the same back-and-forth rhythm, invoices generated through the same steps each month. He noticed how often he made the same decisions repeatedly—clarifying scope, reformatting documents, explaining timelines. He noticed how much of his work was reactive rather than designed, shaped by incoming requests instead of deliberate architecture.

The realization wasn't dramatic. It was quiet and slightly embarrassing. He had optimized effort, but he had not optimized scale.

There is a difference between working efficiently and working beyond yourself. Efficiency makes you faster. Leverage makes you less necessary.

The distinction changed the way Marcus viewed his role. Until then, he had considered himself the engine of the business. If something needed to move, he applied force. Now he began to wonder whether his job was not to push harder, but to build something that moved without constant pressure.

He started small. Instead of drafting onboarding emails from scratch, he mapped the entire onboarding experience from the moment a contract was signed. He identified what information he always requested, what documents he always sent, what calendar coordination always occurred. He wrote it down in full sentences, then reorganized it into a repeatable flow. He built a structured template that automatically pulled in client information from a form. He connected that form to a shared folder system that created itself when triggered. He embedded a scheduling link that adapted around his protected work blocks rather than forcing him into negotiation threads.

The first time he built the system, it took nearly three hours—far longer than manually onboarding a single client. But when the next client signed, the process unfolded with minimal intervention. The email drafted itself with contextual details. The folder structure appeared. The calendar invitation adjusted automatically. Instead of orchestrating each step, Marcus reviewed and approved.

Encouraged, he turned to proposals. Historically, he had treated each proposal as a blank canvas, believing customization equaled care. Yet when he examined ten recent proposals side by side, he saw that the structure was almost identical. The differences lived in scope details, not architecture. He built a modular template that allowed sections to expand or contract depending on client responses. He created a short intake questionnaire and connected it to a drafting workflow that produced a structured first version. Artificial intelligence helped generate preliminary language based on predefined parameters, which he then refined rather than originated.

Over the next three months, the changes accumulated. Scheduling no longer required multi-email negotiations. Follow-ups triggered automatically if a lead failed to respond. Invoices were generated and sent without manual prompting. Status updates pulled from centralized project boards instead of living in his head.

When he reviewed his numbers at the end of the quarter, the shift was measurable. His weekly working hours had dropped from roughly fifty-five to just under forty. The number of clients he could manage increased by more than fifty percent because his attention was no longer consumed by administrative repetition. Reactive time—those hours spent responding to unpredictable requests—had fallen dramatically because many predictable requests were no longer unpredictable. Revenue rose not because he charged more, but because his throughput expanded without proportional strain.

What surprised him most was not the financial improvement. It was the psychological shift. He no longer felt like the fragile center of a spinning system. There were layers beneath him now— automation, templates, logic, invisible infrastructure. Work continued even when he stepped away for an afternoon. For the first time in years, he took a full week off without orchestrating every detail in advance. Nothing collapsed.

This is what it means to move beyond human scale. It is not about becoming superhuman. It is about building structures that extend beyond the limitations of one person's continuous involvement.

But Marcus also encountered new risks as he built. At one point, intoxicated by the promise of automation, he layered tool upon tool without fully understanding how they interacted. When one integration failed silently, several processes broke downstream. A client didn't receive onboarding instructions. A follow-up sequence misfired. He realized then that leverage can collapse under its own complexity. Over-automation creates fragility when systems become too intricate to monitor. Tool sprawl introduces hidden points of failure. Delegation without clarity—whether to a person or a piece of software—can misalign outcomes and quietly erode trust.

He learned that moving beyond human scale requires discipline as much as ambition. Each new layer of automation had to be justified by frequency and stability. Each delegated function required clear inputs and measurable outputs. Each tool had to earn its place in the architecture rather than serve as a distraction disguised as progress.

The lesson was not that effort was obsolete. Effort built the foundation. Skill attracted demand. Discipline sustained the early phase. But beyond a certain threshold, additional effort produced diminishing returns. What unlocked the next stage was design.

Marcus no longer measured productivity by how exhausted he felt at the end of the day. He measured it by how many recurring problems disappeared permanently. Each time a task transformed into a self-sustaining process, he reclaimed a piece of his cognitive bandwidth. Each time a repeated decision became encoded into a template or rule, he reduced the mental load of future weeks.

The ceiling had not disappeared; it had shifted upward. Instead of being constrained by the limits of his hours, he was constrained by the quality of his architecture. That was a constraint he could expand indefinitely.

Beyond human scale is not a slogan. It is a structural reality available to anyone willing to stop equating effort with value and start treating their work as something that can be engineered. The moment you ask not how to complete the task, but how to remove yourself from needing to complete it again, you begin crossing that threshold.

And once you experience work continuing without your constant presence, it becomes impossible to return to the old model.

Chapter 2, The Leverage Equation

The first time Marcus tried to explain what had changed in his business, he defaulted to vague language. He told a friend he had "optimized his systems." He said he was "using more automation." He mentioned AI. But none of it captured the underlying shift. It wasn't that he had adopted better tools. It was that he had started to understand the math behind his output.

For years, he had unconsciously operated under a simple formula, more input equals more output. If he wanted to earn more, he worked more. If he wanted to deliver more, he stayed up later. If he wanted to grow, he accepted more responsibility. The equation was linear, and it felt honest. Effort in, results out.

But once he began redesigning his workflows, he noticed something unsettling. Two hours spent building a structured automation produced more long-term impact than twenty hours of direct execution. A well-designed template replaced weeks of repeated thinking. A single afternoon spent refining a process erased dozens of future interruptions.

The relationship between effort and outcome was not linear. It was multiplicative.

He began to sketch what was happening in clearer terms. Output, he realized, was not simply a function of time. It depended on the quality of his skill, the intensity of his focus, the presence of structural leverage, and the drag imposed by friction. If he were to describe it plainly, the equation looked more like this,

DAVID WEBB

Output equals skill multiplied by focused input, multiplied again by structural leverage, minus friction.

At first glance, the formula appeared abstract. But when he applied it to his own work, it clarified everything.

Skill mattered because leverage amplifies competence, not incompetence. A poorly structured system simply spreads poor judgment at scale. Focused input mattered because distracted work diluted quality before it ever reached a system. Structural leverage—the automations, templates, workflows, integrations—determined whether his effort compounded or evaporated. And friction quietly subtracted from everything.

Friction was the hidden variable he had ignored for years.

It appeared as context switching, as unclear instructions, as manual repetition, as tool conflicts, as unnecessary approvals, as waiting for responses that could have been automated. It manifested in small delays that felt insignificant individually but accumulated into hours of lost cognitive energy. Friction was measurable if he paid attention. Every time he repeated a decision he had already made, friction was present. Every time he searched for a file that should have been automatically organized, friction had taken its toll. Every time a system required maintenance because he had rushed its design, friction was subtracting from his theoretical output.

He began to understand that leverage was not merely something you added. It was something you maintained. And like any multiplier, it could decay.

The first sign of decay appeared when an automation he had built months earlier began misrouting data after a minor software update. For several weeks, he manually corrected errors without investigating the root cause. His output did not collapse, but it subtly degraded. Tasks that once ran invisibly required intervention again. His effective leverage had shrunk, even though the system still technically existed.

Leverage decays when systems are not maintained, when integrations change, when processes evolve without documentation being updated, or when complexity accumulates faster than clarity. The multiplier weakens quietly. If ignored, it can reverse, turning into negative leverage—structures that consume more energy than they save.

This realization pushed Marcus to think in terms of leverage maturity. Not all systems are equal. Not all structures multiply effort in the same way. Some barely reduce friction. Others transform the entire scale of operation.

At the earliest stage, everything is manual. He remembered this phase clearly. Every task required deliberate action. Emails were written from scratch. Files were named individually. Scheduling was negotiated line by line. This was the ground floor of maturity, where skill and effort were the only drivers of output. There was no multiplier.

The next stage emerged when he introduced templates. Proposals followed a defined structure. Emails reused proven language. Onboarding steps followed a documented sequence. The work was still manual, but the thinking behind it was partially pre-encoded. Effort remained necessary, yet cognitive strain dropped. Output increased modestly.

As he layered automation into these templates, he entered a semi-automated stage. Forms populated documents. Calendar links replaced negotiation. Follow-ups triggered automatically. At this level, effort began to detach from execution. He was still present, but less frequently required.

The transformation accelerated when systems began integrating with one another. His CRM updated his project board. His project board triggered billing. Billing updated reporting dashboards. Individual tools were no longer isolated; they communicated. This integration marked a structural shift. He was no longer managing tasks. He was managing flows.

Artificial intelligence introduced another layer. Drafts generated themselves from structured inputs. Meeting transcripts summarized automatically. Data patterns surfaced without manual analysis. AI did not replace judgment, but it accelerated cognition. The system began assisting thought itself.

Eventually, Marcus glimpsed a higher stage—systems that monitored their own performance and adjusted parameters based on feedback. Analytics dashboards highlighted bottlenecks. Engagement metrics informed content scheduling automatically. Certain thresholds triggered notifications before problems became visible. The system was not conscious, but it was adaptive.

These stages represented a spectrum of leverage maturity, from fully manual execution to self-optimizing structures. Each level increased the multiplier in the equation. Each level also increased the risk of mismanagement.

Because leverage, like capital, can be overextended.

At one point, intoxicated by efficiency gains, Marcus adopted three new tools in a single month. Each promised optimization. Each introduced additional integrations. For a brief period, output appeared to spike. Then the cracks surfaced. Two tools overlapped in functionality. Notifications multiplied. Dependencies deepened. Debugging consumed time that exceeded the gains.

He had crossed into diminishing returns.

The paradox of leverage is that more tools do not always equal more scale. Complexity itself introduces friction. When the cognitive load required to manage systems exceeds the effort they save, the equation reverses. Structural leverage becomes structural drag.

Marcus learned to ask a different question before adding any new layer, does this reduce friction more than it introduces? Does it meaningfully increase the multiplier, or merely rearrange effort?

Sometimes the answer was restraint.

He removed redundant tools. Simplified workflows. Consolidated platforms. Each simplification increased clarity, which in turn strengthened leverage. The equation stabilized again.

Over time, he began to see his business less as a series of tasks and more as an evolving mathematical system. Skill development improved the base multiplier. Focused work strengthened the quality of input. Structural leverage amplified the results of both. Friction subtracted from all of it. Maintenance preserved the multiplier. Discipline prevented decay. Simplicity guarded against diminishing returns.

The equation was not theoretical. It was observable.

When he invested deeply in improving his craft, the amplified output of his systems improved accordingly. When he protected focused time and eliminated reactive clutter, the quality of what entered the system rose. When he refined automations and removed unnecessary steps, friction decreased and output climbed without additional hours. When he neglected maintenance, subtle inefficiencies crept in and eroded gains.

For the first time, growth felt predictable.

He no longer chased productivity hacks or temporary bursts of motivation. He evaluated changes through the lens of the equation. Would this improve skill? Would this increase focused input? Would this meaningfully enhance structural leverage? Would this reduce friction? Or would it quietly add complexity?

The clarity was liberating.

The old model had required constant exertion. The new model required design, measurement, and refinement. Effort still mattered, but it was no longer the sole driver of expansion. Effort fed the system. The system multiplied effort. Friction moderated the result.

Beyond a certain point, working harder without strengthening the multiplier simply meant colliding with the ceiling faster.

But strengthening the multiplier changed the ceiling itself.

The Leverage Equation was not a slogan or motivational device. It was a structural reality. Every person operates within it, whether consciously or not. The difference between linear growth and exponential expansion lies in understanding the full equation—and managing each component deliberately.

1. Skill without leverage caps quickly.
2. Leverage without skill magnifies mediocrity.
3. Input without focus wastes potential.
4. Leverage without maintenance decays.
5. Tools without simplicity create drag.

When all components align, output expands beyond what effort alone could ever achieve.

That is the mathematics of moving beyond yourself.

Chapter 3, The Rise of Invisible Teams

When Elena left her agency job to build a solo strategy practice, she told herself she was trading complexity for simplicity. No staff meetings. No internal politics. No payroll. Just her, a laptop, and clients who valued clarity.

For the first six months, the simplicity felt clean. Every email was written by her. Every meeting scheduled by her. Every proposal assembled manually. Every onboarding sequence orchestrated in real time. She was efficient and careful, and because demand was modest, she could afford to manage every detail personally.

Then something changed.

Demand didn't grow gradually; it accelerated. Referrals began stacking. Speaking invitations arrived. A newsletter she had started casually began attracting a serious audience. What had once been manageable now felt volatile. She wasn't overwhelmed because the work was difficult. She was overwhelmed because she had become the routing layer for everything.

Every inquiry passed through her.
Every calendar negotiation required her.
Every document transfer depended on her.
Every follow-up waited for her memory.

She wasn't running a business. She was acting as a switchboard.

The realization unsettled her because she had deliberately chosen not to build a team. She didn't want employees. She didn't want hierarchy. She didn't want the administrative weight that had pushed her out of corporate life in the first place.

What she hadn't realized was that there was another option.

The first shift happened accidentally. After missing a scheduling request buried in her inbox, she decided to restructure how meetings were arranged. Instead of negotiating availability through back-and-forth emails, she implemented a dynamic scheduling layer that reflected her actual working preferences. It respected deep work blocks. It automatically adjusted time zones. It confirmed appointments and sent reminders without further involvement.

The result was subtle but profound. Calendar coordination ceased to consume attention. The role that had quietly existed inside her head—full-time scheduler—had been externalized.

That was the first member of her invisible team.

Once she noticed it, she began seeing other roles she had been unconsciously performing. When a client completed an intake form, they manually transferred information into multiple systems. She updated her CRM. She created a project folder. She generated an invoice draft. She sent onboarding instructions. None of these actions required strategic thought. They required reliability.

So she built a data routing layer. Information entered once and flowed automatically into every relevant system. Records updated themselves. Folders generated. Status boards reflected real-time progress. The silent administrative assistant she had been impersonating disappeared.

The second member of her invisible team had emerged, the data router.

Next, she examined how her content moved through the world. Writing a weekly article required not just drafting, but formatting, distribution, repurposing, and archiving. Each step was small. Together they consumed hours. She designed a distribution architecture in which one completed piece triggered a chain reaction, formatting adapted to each channel, summaries generated automatically, archives updated, metrics logged. The work of a marketing coordinator became encoded in structure.

A third invisible role took shape, the content distributor.

Client onboarding, once a personalized but repetitive ritual, became a defined experience. The moment a contract was signed, a cascade of structured actions unfolded. Welcome materials were delivered. Expectations were clarified. Shared spaces were provisioned. Timelines were visible. The emotional weight of remembering every nuance vanished because the process itself remembered.

The fourth role—the onboarding manager—was no longer dependent on her mood or availability.

Finally, she confronted the blind spot she had ignored, measurement. Previously, she evaluated progress sporadically, pulling data manually when something felt off. She built dashboards that surfaced leading indicators automatically. Engagement patterns, pipeline health, revenue flow, client timelines—all visible without prompting. When anomalies appeared, she was alerted early rather than discovering them late.

The fifth role, the analytics monitor, completed the structure.

What Elena had constructed was not a collection of tools. It was an architecture. Information entered the system through defined inputs, forms, emails, payments, content drafts. That information passed through a processing layer composed of logic rules, automations, and integrations. Outputs emerged in the form of scheduled meetings, updated records, distributed content, invoices, confirmations. Beneath it all, a feedback layer measured performance, logged activity, and signaled exceptions.

Input flowed into processing. Processing produced output. Output generated feedback. Feedback refined the next cycle.

She no longer experienced her work as a series of isolated actions. She experienced it as a living system.

The psychological shift was immediate. She stopped feeling like the center of activity. Instead, she felt like the designer of an environment that functioned continuously. Work happened while she slept. Clients progressed without reminders. Content traveled without supervision. Decisions became clearer because operational noise had receded.

Yet with scale came a new risk.

One afternoon, an integration between two core systems failed silently after a platform update. For several days, client intake data did not route correctly. Nothing catastrophic occurred, but small inconsistencies began surfacing. A missing folder. An untriggered notification. A slight delay in onboarding.

It was her first encounter with structural fragility.

Invisible teams require trust, and trust requires safeguards. She realized that systems need redundancy, alternative pathways when one connection fails. They require alerting mechanisms so that silent breakdowns become visible quickly. They demand manual override options, allowing her to intervene when automation misfires. And they need logging, clear records of what executed and what did not, so that diagnosis is possible.

Without these safeguards, leverage becomes brittle.

She also noticed a subtler vulnerability, concentration risk. As she consolidated her architecture onto a few powerful platforms, she increased efficiency but also dependency. A single point of failure could cascade widely. An API change could disrupt multiple workflows simultaneously. The convenience of integration masked the exposure it created.

The invisible team was powerful, but it was not infallible.

Elena learned to audit her architecture regularly. Where was she over-reliant on a single vendor? Which processes lacked backup pathways? What would happen if a core tool vanished overnight? The goal was not paranoia. It was resilience.

The maturity of an invisible team is not measured solely by how much it automates, but by how gracefully it absorbs disruption.

Over time, Elena noticed something remarkable. She could handle double the client load she once managed without increasing stress. Not because she had become faster, but because she was no longer performing five invisible jobs simultaneously. The scheduler, the data router, the distributor, the onboarding manager, and the analyst operated continuously in the background.

There was no payroll. No office. No internal meetings.

Yet structurally, she was no longer alone.

The idea that software replaces headcount can sound exaggerated until you define headcount in terms of roles rather than people. Many organizational roles exist to move information predictably from one state to another. When those transitions are encoded into systems, the role persists without requiring a body.

This is the rise of invisible teams.

It is not a rejection of human collaboration. It is a recognition that much of what once required coordination now requires design. The founder's task is no longer to execute every step personally, nor to hire prematurely, but to identify recurring roles within their own workflow and externalize them into architecture.

The moment you stop asking, "Who should I hire for this?" and begin asking, "What role is this, and can it be systematized?" the terrain changes.

But so does responsibility.

Because once the team is invisible, you cannot manage it through conversation. You manage it through structure, monitoring, and intentional simplicity. You build not just for scale, but for stability. You resist the temptation to layer tools endlessly. You choose clarity over novelty.

The invisible team is not magic. It is engineered. And when engineered thoughtfully, it allows one person to operate at a scale that once required many—without inheriting the fragility of constant human coordination.

Beyond human scale is not achieved by replacing yourself with people alone. It is achieved by replacing predictable roles with reliable systems and then supervising the architecture rather than performing the tasks.

That is how a team of one becomes structurally plural.

Chapter 4, Energy Is the Limiter, Not Time

When Daniel finally cleared his calendar for a full "strategy day," he expected relief.

For months, he had been telling himself that the problem was time. Too many meetings. Too many interruptions. Too many small obligations scattered across the week. If he could just carve out an uninterrupted day, he would redesign his offers, rethink his positioning, and map the next phase of growth.

The day arrived. His calendar was empty.

By 10,30 a.m., he felt strangely dull.

He opened a blank document to outline a new product. Nothing came. He skimmed notes from past client calls. He reread old strategy memos. He checked his email "quickly," even though he had promised himself he wouldn't. By early afternoon, he felt restless and vaguely irritated. The time was available. The clarity was not.

That was the moment he began to understand that time had never been the constraint.

Energy was.

We talk about time as if it is the universal currency of productivity, but time is merely a container. It holds activity. It does not guarantee capacity. Two hours with full cognitive clarity can produce more meaningful output than ten hours in a depleted state. Anyone who has tried to do deep work after a day of fragmented meetings knows this instinctively.

Daniel's mistake was assuming that freeing time automatically restored energy. It didn't. By the time he reached his open day, he had already spent his most valuable cognitive fuel on low-leverage decisions throughout the week. His mornings had been consumed by inbox management, minor scheduling conflicts, reactive Slack threads, and small but draining approvals. Each decision was insignificant on its own. Together, they created a form of invisible taxation.

Research in behavioral psychology calls this decision fatigue. The more choices you make, even trivial ones, the more your mental stamina erodes. The quality of subsequent decisions declines. Cognitive flexibility narrows. Creativity suffers. By the time Daniel sat down to design something new, his neurological resources were partially depleted.

But decision fatigue was only one part of the story.

He also began noticing how often he switched contexts during a normal day. Drafting a proposal, then answering a client question, then reviewing analytics, then checking an invoice, then returning to the proposal. Each shift felt minor, but studies on context switching show that attention does not reset instantly. A residue remains. Part of the mind lingers on the previous task, reducing depth and increasing error rates in the next. The cumulative cost of these transitions is measurable. Productivity researchers have demonstrated that even brief interruptions can significantly extend the time required to complete complex work.

Daniel wasn't short on time. He was hemorrhaging energy.

Once he saw this clearly, he stopped organizing his week around hours and started organizing it around energy types. Not all work required the same cognitive profile, and not all depletion felt the same.

He began to notice four distinct forms of energy in his workflow.

There was creative energy, the kind required to generate original ideas, design new offers, write long-form content, and solve ambiguous problems. It was fragile and finite. It flourished in uninterrupted stretches and collapsed under fragmentation.

There was strategic energy, which was less about invention and more about evaluation. Reviewing data, making directional decisions, refining positioning—these required clarity and perspective but not necessarily raw creativity.

There was administrative energy, the steady attention needed for structured execution, updating systems, processing documents, managing logistics. It was not intellectually demanding but could still drain attention if sustained too long.

And then there was reactive energy, the kind consumed by responding to incoming messages, urgent requests, and unpredictable variables. Reactive work often felt productive because it generated visible motion, but it rarely moved the system forward.

Before this classification, all work felt equal. After it, the hierarchy became obvious.

Creative and strategic energy were the true drivers of long-term growth. Administrative and reactive energy were necessary but should not dominate prime cognitive hours.

This realization forced Daniel to confront another uncomfortable truth, he had been spending his highest-quality mental hours on the lowest-leverage tasks.

He began designing what he came to think of as his energy architecture. Instead of asking what needed to be done first, he asked what kind of energy was available at different points in the day and how it should be allocated. Mornings, when his mind was sharpest, became protected zones for creative and strategic work. Administrative tasks were batched into defined windows later in the day. Reactive communication was constrained to specific intervals rather than allowed to bleed across the entire schedule.

But protection alone was insufficient. He needed routing.

For every recurring task, he asked a simple question, does this deserve my creative energy, my strategic energy, or neither?

If the task required no unique judgment and followed a predictable structure, he looked for automation. If it required human attention but not his specific expertise, he delegated. If it required similar cognitive mode as other tasks, he batched it. If it directly shaped the future direction of his work, he protected it.

Slowly, patterns emerged. Client onboarding moved toward automation and structured templates. Data entry disappeared into integrations. Weekly reporting was batched into a single review block. Deep product design sessions were scheduled deliberately when his cognitive capacity peaked.

The leaks became visible once he knew what to look for.

An open browser tab containing an unfinished draft consumed background attention. A vague commitment without a defined next step generated low-grade anxiety. An unresolved client ambiguity lingered in working memory, subtly draining emotional bandwidth. Psychologists refer to this as attention residue and open loop tension—the mind's tendency to hold unresolved items in partial awareness, reducing capacity for new tasks.

He realized that many of his energy leaks were not large problems but incomplete structures. When a task had no defined system, it lived in his head. And anything that lives in your head occupies energy whether you are actively working on it or not.

Emotional bandwidth, he discovered, was equally finite. Every unclear expectation, every ambiguous deadline, every delayed response carried emotional weight. It is exhausting to operate in an environment where outcomes depend on constant vigilance. When systems clarified expectations and automated confirmations, the emotional burden lightened. He stopped wondering whether something had slipped through the cracks because the system itself signaled completion.

Energy architecture, then, was not merely about scheduling. It was about structural conservation.

He began auditing his week through a new lens. Where did creative energy peak? Where did it collapse? Which tasks consistently left him mentally drained for hours afterward? Which activities restored clarity? Instead of tracking time spent, he tracked energy aftereffects.

Within months, the difference was tangible. The same number of hours produced more meaningful output. Product development accelerated. Decision-making sharpened. Even leisure felt different because he was no longer carrying as many unresolved loops as possible in the background.

The paradox was that he had not increased discipline. He had reduced unnecessary expenditure.

Time, he realized, is democratic. Everyone receives twenty-four hours. Energy is not. It fluctuates with sleep, stress, cognitive load, and environment. The mistake most professionals make is treating energy as infinite until proven otherwise. By the time depletion becomes obvious, the damage has already been done.

Artificial leverage is often discussed in terms of tools and automation. But its deeper function is energy preservation. Every automated reminder protects a fragment of cognitive bandwidth. Every delegated workflow removes a decision. Every batched communication window reduces context switching. Every protected deep work block safeguards creative fuel.

When you stop asking how to fit more tasks into your day and start asking how to design your work so that high-value energy is spent only where it compounds, productivity shifts from effort to architecture.

Daniel's open calendar day eventually produced the strategy he had hoped for—but not because he cleared time. It worked because he had redesigned the weeks leading up to it. His mind arrived rested, unfragmented, and structurally supported.

Energy, not time, had been the limiter all along.

And once he built his systems to conserve it, the ceiling rose.

Chapter 5, The Systems-First Mindset

For a long time, Priya believed she was being responsible.

Every time a client request came in, she handled it immediately. When a small issue appeared in her workflow, she fixed it on the spot. When something broke, she patched it quickly and moved on. Her responsiveness was one of the reasons clients trusted her. She prided herself on speed.

But she began noticing something uncomfortable. The same types of issues kept resurfacing. The same onboarding confusion. The same proposal adjustments. The same follow-up reminders that required manual nudging. Each instance was small enough to fix in minutes. None felt worth "building a system" around.

And yet, over a year, those minutes accumulated into weeks.

What she was experiencing was not inefficiency. It was structural immaturity.

A systems-first mindset does not ask whether a task can be completed. It asks whether it should ever need to be completed manually again. The shift is subtle but decisive. It moves attention away from immediate resolution and toward permanent elimination of recurrence.

Priya's breakthrough came when she reviewed her calendar across three months instead of one week. Patterns emerged immediately. Client onboarding required nearly identical steps each time. Proposal formatting varied only superficially. Weekly reporting followed the same sequence. Even her responses to common objections were 80 percent identical.

She had been solving the same problems repeatedly.

From that observation, she developed a personal threshold, if she performed a task five times in roughly the same way, it was no longer a task. It was a candidate for systemization.

The "Five Repeats Rule," as she later called it, forced her to slow down. The first time something happened, she handled it. The second and third times, she paid attention. By the fifth instance, she stopped and asked a different question, what structure would prevent this from living in my head again?

Systemization, she discovered, unfolds in stages. At the most basic level, nothing is documented. Every action relies on memory. She recognized this as her starting point—pure manual execution. The work existed only in her mind and her habits.

The first step upward was documentation. Writing down the exact sequence of actions required to complete a recurring task felt trivial, even bureaucratic. But once the process was externalized, she could examine it objectively. Hidden redundancies surfaced. Ambiguities became visible. Documentation alone reduced cognitive load because she no longer needed to reconstruct the process from memory each time.

From documentation emerged templating. Instead of referencing instructions and rebuilding from scratch, she created structured starting points. Email drafts, proposal frameworks, onboarding checklists—all pre-formed but adaptable. The mental cost of beginning dropped significantly.

Automation followed naturally. When she identified parts of the template that were purely mechanical—copying information from one place to another, sending scheduled reminders, generating recurring reports—she encoded them into workflows. Tasks no longer required initiation; they triggered themselves based on defined conditions.

But she soon realized that isolated automations only solved local inefficiencies. True leverage emerged when separate processes began communicating. When client intake forms populated her CRM, which updated her project board, which triggered invoicing, she moved beyond automation into integration. The system behaved as a coordinated whole rather than a collection of fragments.

The final stage was monitoring. She installed simple oversight mechanisms that signaled when something deviated from expectation. Reports surfaced weekly without prompting. Exceptions triggered alerts. Instead of wondering whether processes had executed, she had visibility. The system did not merely run; it informed.

Over time, Priya began seeing these stages as a ladder. At the base was full manual execution. Above it, documentation created clarity. Templates reduced cognitive strain. Automation removed repetitive motion. Integration connected isolated efficiencies into coherent flows. Monitoring ensured resilience.

Not every task deserved to climb to the highest rung. The ladder was a tool for judgment, not a mandate for maximal automation. Some processes benefited enormously from integration and monitoring. Others were sufficiently served by a well-designed template.

The mistake she had made previously was evaluating systemization through the lens of immediate effort. Writing documentation felt slower than simply doing the task. Building automation took longer than executing manually. But once she began quantifying the return, the math became obvious.

She started calculating what she informally called system return on investment. For any recurring task, she estimated how much time it consumed per occurrence, how frequently it happened, and how long she expected to perform it in her business lifecycle. Multiplying those variables revealed the total future time cost. From that total, she subtracted the hours required to design the system. If the net result was positive—and it almost always was—the investment justified itself.

One onboarding process, for example, took forty minutes per client. With an average of four new clients per month, which was over thirty hours per year. Designing a structured workflow took three hours. The return was immediate and compounded annually. When she extended this calculation across multiple recurring processes, the cumulative savings were staggering.

More importantly, the savings were not merely temporal. They were cognitive. Each systemized process removed a recurring decision. Decision fatigue diminished. Attention residue shrank. Emotional friction decreased because fewer tasks depended on memory or vigilance.

The more she applied this mindset, the more her work began to resemble architecture rather than activity. She no longer celebrated completing tasks. She celebrated eliminating categories of tasks permanently.

What surprised her was how quickly the effects compounded. Once onboarding was systemized, scaling client volume did not proportionally increase workload. When proposals were templated and automated, response time shortened while effort decreased. When reporting integrated automatically, client transparency improved without additional labor.

The firefighting impulse that once defined her days gradually disappeared, not because problems ceased, but because recurring problems had been structurally neutralized.

There was, however, a danger in overenthusiasm. At one point, she attempted to systemize an irregular creative process that required nuance and improvisation. The resulting structure felt rigid and counterproductive. She learned that systemization should target repetition and predictability, not artistry or strategic judgment. Forcing every activity onto the ladder risks suffocating the very elements that create differentiation.

The systems-first mindset, properly applied, does not replace thought. It preserves it. It removes the need to repeatedly think about what does not require new thinking.

Over time, Priya stopped viewing system design as overhead. It became her primary form of leverage. Instead of asking how much she accomplished each week, she began asking how many future weeks had become easier because of something she built today.

That reframing changed her sense of progress. Growth no longer meant more activity. It meant greater structural maturity.

Manual work had built her competence. Systems built her capacity.

And once capacity became decoupled from constant execution, the scale of what she could sustain expanded without strain.

Chapter 6, Thinking Like a Toolmaker

When Adrian first started building online products, he thought tools were something you downloaded.

He experimented constantly. New project management software. New writing apps. New automation platforms. Every few months he migrated to something better, faster, more elegant. He believed optimization meant discovering superior tools.

But despite the upgrades, his workflow felt strangely unchanged. Tasks still required effort. Decisions still repeated. Bottlenecks still appeared. The tools had improved, but his output had not multiplied.

The shift began the day he stopped asking which tool to use and started asking what tool he needed to exist.

That distinction changed everything.

Most people operate as tool users. They accept the structure of whatever software they adopt. They adapt their workflow to the platform. They squeeze their processes into predefined templates. When friction appears, they tolerate it.

Toolmakers do the opposite. They adapt tools to their workflow. They treat platforms as raw material. They shape the environment around the way they think and operate.

The psychological difference is subtle but decisive. A tool user asks, "How do I use this feature?" A toolmaker asks, "What recurring friction in my work could be encoded into something reusable?"

Adrian began paying attention to friction. Not dramatic obstacles—small, recurring annoyances. Rewriting similar sales emails. Manually formatting weekly reports. Reorganizing research notes. Explaining the same onboarding instructions to clients. Each instance was minor. Together, they represented invisible drag.

Instead of fixing each occurrence individually, he began identifying patterns. That was the first move, noticing repetition with precision. If something happened often enough to feel familiar, it qualified as friction worth studying.

The next step was abstraction. He would strip away surface differences and search for the underlying structure. Ten different client emails might look distinct, but beneath them lay the same components, acknowledgment, clarification, timeline, next step. Five different proposal documents might vary in language, but they shared identical architecture.

Abstraction revealed the pattern behind the instance.

Once he understood the pattern, he defined inputs. What information was actually variable? Client name, project scope, deadline, pricing tier. Everything else was stable. By separating variables from constants, he transformed messy documents into structured frameworks.

From there, he built templates—not static forms, but flexible structures that accepted defined inputs and generated predictable outputs. A proposal template with modular sections. An email response structure with interchangeable blocks. A reporting format that pulled from standardized data fields.

But templating alone was not enough. Where mechanical repetition remained, he introduced automation. If data was being copied between systems, it should move automatically. If reminders were sent on a predictable schedule, they should trigger themselves. If a document could be generated from structured input, it should be assembled without manual formatting.

He tested each new structure in real conditions. The first version rarely worked perfectly. Edge cases appeared.

Assumptions failed. He refined, adjusted, simplified. Refinement was not optional; it was the stage that separated durable tools from fragile hacks.

Finally, he integrated the tool into the broader system. A template that lives in isolation still requires memory. But once embedded within a workflow—triggered by a form submission, linked to a CRM, connected to a task board—it becomes part of a coordinated architecture.

This progression—from identifying friction to integrating refined tools into systems—became his default mode of operation.

Over time, Adrian realized that most people confuse tools with systems. A tool is a capability. It performs a specific function. A calendar schedules. A document editor formats text. An automation platform moves data.

A system, by contrast, is coordinated logic across multiple tools with defined flow. It has inputs, processing rules, outputs, and feedback. A scheduling tool becomes part of a system when it connects to onboarding workflows, billing triggers, and reminder sequences. A document template becomes part of a system when it is automatically populated, stored, tracked, and analyzed.

Tools execute tasks. Systems execute outcomes.

Understanding that difference prevented him from romanticizing complexity. Buying a new tool did not equate to building leverage. Only when that tool was embedded within coherent flow did it multiply output.

Artificial intelligence accelerated this mindset dramatically.

Initially, he treated AI as a novelty—something to generate drafts or summarize notes. But once he began thinking like a toolmaker, he recognized AI as malleable clay.

He stopped issuing one-off prompts and began constructing structured input patterns. Instead of writing, "Draft a proposal," he created parameterized prompts that accepted defined variables—industry, objective, tone, constraints—and produced consistent frameworks. He stored these prompts in organized libraries, refining language with each iteration. He versioned them, preserving improvements rather than overwriting past experiments.

AI became a component within his broader toolmaking process. It helped abstract patterns from previous work. It generated structured first drafts from templated inputs. It analyzed recurring objections and suggested refinements. But it never replaced design. It amplified it.

The difference was visible in his output. Instead of staring at blank pages, he interacted with structured drafts. Instead of rewriting repetitive content, he reviewed and refined. Instead of improvising responses, he triggered established frameworks.

But he also encountered the danger of over-automation. At one point, he attempted to automate a nuanced client strategy process that depended heavily on contextual judgment. The output became technically correct but strategically shallow. He learned that not every cognitive activity benefits from templating. Toolmaking should remove repetition, not flatten insight.

He began applying a simple filter. If a task required novel reasoning every time, it deserved human attention. If it required predictable structure, it deserved tooling.

The cumulative effect of this approach was not simply efficiency. It was identity transformation. Adrian stopped seeing himself primarily as a producer of output and started seeing himself as a builder of capabilities. Each refined template, each integrated workflow, each structured prompt became a reusable asset. Problems solved once stayed solved.

This shift also changed his tolerance for friction. He no longer accepted small inefficiencies as the cost of doing business. Each recurring annoyance was a signal. Each signal pointed to a potential tool waiting to be built.

He did not need to write software from scratch to be a toolmaker. Modern platforms provided raw materials. Visual automation builders allowed logic without code. AI systems enabled pattern recognition and generation without deep programming knowledge. The barrier was no longer technical ability; it was intentional design.

Over time, the compounding effect became undeniable. Weeks that once felt dense with minor obligations grew spacious. Creative sessions began faster because structural preparation had already occurred. Administrative work shrank because many transitions executed automatically.

The ultimate realization was this, the highest leverage skill in the modern era is not using tools efficiently. It is shaping them around your specific context.

Anyone can download an app. Few people build an ecosystem that reflects how they think.

Thinking like a toolmaker does not require genius. It requires observation, abstraction, and the patience to encode patterns into structure. Once you adopt that orientation, every recurring action becomes an opportunity. Every friction point becomes raw material.

And gradually, the world you work inside begins to feel less like something you manage and more like something you engineered.

That is when leverage stops being theoretical and becomes structural.

Chapter 7, Modern Leverage, Capital, Code, and Content

When Noah's consulting business plateaued, his instinct was to work harder.

Revenue had stabilized. Client satisfaction was high. But growth had flattened. He responded the way most competent operators do—by increasing input. He reached out to more prospects. He experimented with new offers. He extended his working hours slightly. For a few months, the numbers ticked upward again.

Then they stalled. The problem was not effort. It was leverage composition.

For years, Noah had been relying primarily on one form of leverage without realizing it, his own code-like systems. He had built strong automations, efficient workflows, structured onboarding, integrated reporting. His operational backbone was solid. But his reach was limited, and his ability to accelerate outcomes was constrained by the speed at which his systems could compound organically.

He began to see that modern leverage exists in three distinct but interconnected currencies, capital, code, and content.

Capital is stored momentum. It is money deployed to compress time. Code is embedded logic. It performs work repeatedly without additional human effort. Content is distributed thought. It multiplies voice and authority across distance and duration.

Individually, each has power. Together, they form a compounding architecture.

Noah's bias toward code had made him operationally elegant but commercially conservative. He hesitated to deploy capital aggressively. He produced content sporadically. His systems were strong, but they were amplifying a narrow stream of demand.

To understand how to rebalance, he reframed each currency in structural terms.

Capital, he realized, is not merely spending. It is acceleration. When deployed precisely, it replaces waiting. Instead of slowly building reach organically, capital can purchase distribution. Instead of manually learning a new skill over months, capital can secure expertise. Instead of tolerating inefficient infrastructure, capital can upgrade it immediately.

But capital is blunt when clarity is absent. He had once spent thousands on advertising before refining his offer. Traffic increased, but conversions did not. Money amplified ambiguity. The result was not growth, but amplified inefficiency.

Capital without clarity is waste.

Code, by contrast, is disciplined repetition. It transforms variable human effort into consistent mechanical execution. Noah's automated workflows, data routing systems, and structured templates were forms of code. They did not require additional payroll to scale. Once configured, they executed at near-zero marginal cost.

But code carries its own risk. At one point, he layered so many interconnected automations that troubleshooting became complex. When a small integration broke, the ripple effects spread widely. The system was powerful, but fragile.

Code without simplicity becomes brittle.

Content operates differently. It is neither stored money nor embedded logic. It is stored thinking. A well-articulated idea, published once, can attract attention for years. Content scales authority and trust in ways neither capital nor code can replicate directly. It extends influence beyond immediate networks.

When Noah committed to consistent content production—clear frameworks, case studies, strategic insights—his inbound demand shifted. Clients began referencing specific articles during sales calls. Trust accelerated. His sales cycle shortened. The content acted as a silent advocate.

But content also decays. Without distribution, it becomes noise. Without structure, it becomes scattered. Without integration into a larger system, it generates attention without conversion.

Content without distribution is static.

Gradually, Noah saw that the three currencies were not interchangeable; they were situational.

When his primary constraint was time—too many manual hours per unit of output—the answer was code. Automate. Integrate. Structure.

When his primary constraint was reach—too few qualified prospects—the answer was content. Publish. Clarify. Distribute.

When his primary constraint was speed—an opportunity window closing quickly—the answer was capital. Invest to accelerate.

When his primary constraint was a skill gap—something beyond his expertise—the solution lay in either capital or code. He could hire competence temporarily, or he could build systems that reduced the skill requirement structurally.

This became his decision lens. Instead of defaulting to effort, he asked which constraint dominated and which currency addressed it most efficiently.

The deeper insight emerged when he stopped viewing these levers independently and began mapping their interaction.

Capital can fund code. Investing in infrastructure reduces future operational cost. Capital can amplify content through paid distribution. Code can distribute content automatically, routing articles to multiple channels, segmenting audiences, triggering follow-ups. Content can generate revenue that replenishes capital. Revenue can then finance improved code.

In isolation, each currency grows linearly. In combination, they compound.

He visualized it as a cycle. Capital accelerates infrastructure. Infrastructure distributes content. Content generates trust and demand. Demand generates revenue. Revenue replenishes capital. Each turn strengthens the next.

But cycles can also spin out of control.

He saw peers overinvest in capital prematurely, buying sophisticated tools and expensive distribution before clarifying positioning. He saw others obsess over code, endlessly refining automations without improving offer quality or audience growth. He saw creators publish relentlessly without building backend systems to capture or convert attention.

Imbalance leads to stagnation.

The discipline, then, was not to maximize one currency, but to align them with strategic phase.

In early stages, content often dominates because trust must be established. In operational scaling phases, code becomes critical to preserve margins and reduce burnout. During expansion windows, capital compresses timelines.

The mistake most operators make is romanticizing one lever. Some glorify bootstrapping and reject capital entirely. Others worship automation and neglect message clarity. Still others chase visibility without structural backend.

Noah began conducting periodic leverage audits. Where was friction highest? Where was opportunity greatest? Was he constrained by attention, execution capacity, or acceleration speed? Each answer pointed toward a different lever.

Over time, he noticed something counterintuitive. The more precisely he deployed capital, the less of it he needed. The more elegantly he built code, the simpler his architecture became. The more intentionally he created content, the less noise he produced.

Leverage matured not through accumulation, but through calibration.

The triad of capital, code, and content is not a slogan. It is a structural framework for diagnosing growth. When output stalls, the question is not "How can I work harder?" but "Which lever is underdeveloped relative to my constraint?"

When properly balanced, the three amplify one another. Capital accelerates code. Code distributes content. Content replenishes capital. The loop tightens. Effort decouples from scale.

But the loop only compounds when clarity governs deployment. Otherwise, money leaks, systems fracture, and attention dissipates.

The modern operator who understands this triad stops chasing random improvements. Instead, they strengthen the weakest currency relative to their current bottleneck. They invest not emotionally, but strategically.

And as the currencies begin reinforcing one another, growth stops feeling forced.

It starts feeling engineered.

Chapter 8, Delegation Without Dependency

When Omar hired his first assistant, he expected relief.

For months, he had been juggling client delivery, invoicing, scheduling, follow-ups, and content publishing alone. Everyone told him the same thing, just delegate. Once you get help, everything opens up.

The first week felt promising. Tasks left his plate. His inbox thinned. His calendar breathed.

By the third week, the relief had turned into a different kind of pressure.

His assistant messaged frequently for clarification. Deadlines slipped because expectations had not been fully specified. Work came back requiring revision. Omar found himself reviewing, correcting, and re-explaining more than he had anticipated. The tasks were technically off his plate, but mentally they remained his responsibility.

He had delegated tasks. He had not delegated structure.

Delegation without structure is abdication. And abdication creates hidden dependency.

The mistake Omar made was assuming that handing off activity equaled removing responsibility. In reality, he had transferred execution but retained ambiguity. The outcome was not autonomy; it was diffusion.

He began to see that effective delegation is architectural, not conversational. It requires clarity before transfer, not correction after failure.

The first shift happened when he stopped asking, "Can you handle this?" and began asking, "Have I defined this well enough that it can be handled without me?"

He reviewed a recurring task he had delegated, client onboarding coordination. Previously, he had simply said, "Please onboard new clients when contracts are signed." That instruction assumed shared context. It assumed understanding of tone, timeline, document order, edge cases.

So he rebuilt the handoff.

He defined the desired outcome explicitly. A fully onboarded client meant that welcome materials were sent, shared folders created, kickoff calls scheduled, billing initiated, and project boards populated. He clarified how success would be measured— no missed steps, no duplicate communications, no delayed scheduling beyond twenty-four hours.

He documented context. Why each step mattered. Where information lived. What tone to use in communication. He removed implicit knowledge and made it visible.

Finally, he defined escalation triggers. If a client requested scope changes, if payment failed, if required information was incomplete, the task should return to him immediately. Otherwise, it should proceed without interruption.

What he had unknowingly built was a readiness filter. Before delegating anything, he now asked himself whether the outcome was clearly defined, whether success could be objectively measured, whether sufficient context existed in writing, and whether boundaries for escalation were explicit.

If any of those conditions failed, delegation would fail.

This filter slowed him down at first. It required thinking through the work before transferring it. But once he internalized it, the quality of delegation improved dramatically.

He also realized that delegation requires architecture beyond clarity.

A task handed off verbally still depends on memory. A task embedded within a defined structure gains independence.

He began constructing what he thought of as delegation architecture. Each recurring delegated function required five components. First, a standard operating procedure—a clear description of steps, inputs, and outputs. Second, a template—pre-built formats that eliminated ambiguity in execution. Third, a trigger—a defined event that initiated the task automatically, whether a contract signature, a form submission, or a status change in a system. Fourth, feedback—a mechanism for confirming completion or surfacing anomalies. And fifth, audit—periodic review to ensure quality remained aligned with expectations.

Without an SOP, delegation depended on interpretation. Without templates, variation crept in. Without triggers, tasks required reminders. Without feedback, errors went unnoticed. Without audit, standards decayed.

When these components were in place, something changed. His assistant stopped asking routine clarification questions. Onboarding proceeded without intervention. Invoices went out on schedule. Weekly reporting assembled itself and awaited review rather than instruction.

The relationship shifted from dependency to trust. But trust, Omar discovered, requires boundaries.

Early on, he had oscillated between micromanagement and over-detachment. When he reviewed every small detail obsessively, he undermined autonomy. When he withdrew completely, he lost visibility.

The solution was an escalation tree.

He defined clearly which decisions belonged entirely to the delegated role, which required notification but not approval, and which required his explicit involvement before proceeding. Routine scheduling changes required no input. Minor client clarifications required notification. Contractual modifications or scope expansions required approval.

By mapping decision thresholds in advance, he eliminated ambiguity about when work should flow back to him. Escalation became structured rather than emotional.

This also exposed a deeper psychological barrier.

Many founders resist structured delegation not because they lack systems, but because they equate control with involvement. Being needed feels validating. Approving everything reinforces identity as the linchpin. But the more Omar encoded his thinking into documents, templates, and decision trees, the less indispensable he became in day-to-day execution.

Initially, that felt uncomfortable. Then it felt powerful.

He began noticing how much cognitive bandwidth freed up when he was no longer the bottleneck for routine decisions. Strategic thinking improved. Long-term planning resurfaced. Creative energy returned.

Delegation, properly structured, did not reduce his influence. It amplified it.

Yet he also encountered failure.

At one point, he delegated a complex strategic analysis task without sufficient documentation. The assistant completed it competently but misaligned with his underlying intent. The revision process consumed more time than performing it himself would have.

The lesson was clear, not every task is ready for delegation. Some work requires internal clarity before it can be externalized. Delegation readiness depends on the maturity of the process itself. If the founder cannot describe success precisely, no delegate can execute it consistently.

Over time, Omar stopped viewing delegation as a staffing decision and began seeing it as a systems decision. Whether the execution layer was a human assistant, a contractor, or a piece of software mattered less than whether the structure surrounding the role was complete.

Delegation without architecture creates chaos. Delegation with architecture creates scale.

The final shift occurred when he realized that every successful delegation permanently increased his capacity. Each role externalized from his nervous system reduced internal friction. Each structured handoff eliminated recurring decisions.

He no longer asked how much he could personally handle. He asked how many processes he could design to run independently.

Delegation, then, is not the act of removing yourself from the work. It is the act of embedding your standards into a structure that executes without you.

When that structure exists, dependency dissolves. What remains is leverage.

Chapter 9, The Myth of the Superhuman Founder

When Leah launched her startup, exhaustion felt like proof.

She answered messages at midnight. She reviewed contracts at dawn. She joined every sales call, approved every design decision, rewrote every line of copy. Investors praised her intensity. Clients admired her responsiveness. Her team saw her as unstoppable.

For a while, the company grew quickly. Revenue climbed. New partnerships formed. Momentum built around her energy.

But something else was building too.

Every decision, large or small, flowed upward. Every unusual request waited for her input. Every strategic pivot required her presence in the room. The company did not move without her permission, and because of that, it moved at the speed of her availability.

She was the engine. She was also the ceiling.

The cultural narrative around founders glorifies this phase. We admire the operator who outworks everyone else, who absorbs pressure personally, who refuses to delegate critical functions. But what looks like strength in early stages becomes structural fragility as complexity increases.

Leah discovered this the hard way when she attempted to take her first extended break in three years. Within days, questions accumulated. A partnership stalled because no one felt authorized to negotiate terms. A pricing exception lingered because approval required her judgment. Marketing paused because final messaging always passed through her voice.

Nothing collapsed dramatically. It simply slowed.

The myth of the superhuman founder is not that hard work is ineffective. Hard work is often necessary in early stages. The myth is that intensity scales.

It does not.

There are measurable differences between companies built on hustle and companies built on leverage systems. Hustle-driven models often show early growth but increasing volatility. Decision fatigue rises with headcount. Cycle times lengthen as complexity accumulates. Recovery time after founder absence extends dramatically.

Leverage-driven models behave differently. As systems mature, marginal workload per new client decreases. Decision velocity increases because recurring decisions are encoded into frameworks. Recovery time shortens because operations are structurally distributed. Founder involvement becomes strategic rather than constant.

Leah began examining her role more clinically. She mapped her evolution as a founder across stages.

In the earliest stage, she was purely an operator. She did the work directly. Sales, delivery, operations—everything flowed through her hands. At that stage, intensity was an asset because the organization was small and the feedback loops were short.

As revenue grew, she became an optimizer. She improved processes, shortened response times, refined messaging. But she still remained deeply embedded in execution. Optimization made her faster, but it did not remove dependency.

The next transition was uncomfortable. She began building systems intentionally. Recurring sales conversations were documented and structured. Approval thresholds were defined. Client onboarding became automated. Decision criteria were written explicitly rather than held implicitly. She moved from improving tasks to redesigning flows.

Finally, she reached a stage where her primary role was architectural. She evaluated systems, not individual tasks. She monitored leading indicators rather than reacting to daily noise. She intervened selectively, guided by escalation protocols rather than instinct. The organization no longer required her presence to function; it required her perspective to evolve.

These stages—operator, optimizer, system builder, strategic architect—are not titles. They are modes of maturity. Many founders remain trapped in the second stage indefinitely, optimizing personal performance while avoiding structural redesign. The result is predictable, burnout masked as dedication.

Leah conducted what she later called a bottleneck diagnostic.

She calculated the percentage of decisions that required her direct approval. It was over seventy percent. She measured how many outputs—client deliverables, published content, finalized contracts—depended on her personal touch. Nearly all major ones did. She tracked recovery time after a short three-day absence. It took nearly a week for operations to stabilize fully.

The data was not flattering. The issue was not competence. It was centralization.

A founder becomes a bottleneck when decisions, outputs, and authority converge excessively at a single point. In early stages, centralization is efficient. In growth stages, it becomes restrictive.

Leah began systematically decentralizing without abandoning standards. She defined decision frameworks so that recurring judgments could be made consistently without her presence. She clarified what constituted acceptable variation versus strategic risk. She established clear thresholds for when issues should escalate upward and when they should resolve locally.

Metrics began to shift.

Decision cycles shortened because fewer items waited in her queue. Team confidence increased because authority was explicit rather than implied. Client turnaround improved because processes were structured rather than improvised. Most importantly, she could step away without destabilizing momentum.

The difference between hustle and leverage became quantifiable.

Under the hustle model, adding ten new clients increased her working hours proportionally. Under the leverage model, adding ten new clients increased system throughput with marginal additional founder involvement. Revenue growth decoupled from exhaustion.

The myth persists because hustle is visible. Long hours are easy to observe. Systems are quiet. Architectural improvements do not generate dramatic stories. But the numbers tell a clearer narrative. Leverage systems outperform hustle not because they avoid effort, but because they redirect it toward structure.

There is another psychological layer beneath this transition.

Founders often resist becoming less necessary because necessity feels like validation. If everything depends on you, you matter. Releasing control can feel like diminishing identity. But structural independence does not reduce importance; it changes its nature. Instead of being the constant responder, the founder becomes the strategic calibrator.

Leah noticed that as she reduced daily intervention, her thinking deepened. She spent more time on positioning, partnerships, product evolution. The company grew not through frantic motion, but through intentional expansion.

Burnout did not disappear entirely. Growth always introduces tension. But the tension shifted from personal overload to systemic refinement.

The superhuman founder narrative offers short-term admiration. The strategic architect model offers long-term durability.

When Leah finally took a two-week break, something remarkable happened. Operations continued. Minor issues resolved within defined boundaries. Escalations occurred only when thresholds were crossed. Recovery time upon return was measured in hours, not days.

She was no longer the engine. She was the designer of engines.

The path away from the myth is not moral or ideological. It is structural. It requires mapping your current stage honestly. It requires measuring how centralized your decisions remain. It requires reducing dependency deliberately rather than reactively.

The founder who evolves does not abandon intensity. They reassign it. Instead of pouring effort into doing everything personally, they invest it into building systems that reduce personal necessity.

And once that shift occurs, growth stops feeling like self-sacrifice.

It begins to feel sustainable.

Chapter 10, Working at Strategic Altitude

On Tuesday mornings, before the inbox opened and before the dashboards refreshed, Julian did something that once felt irresponsible.

He stopped working.

Not in the casual sense of scrolling or drifting, but in the deliberate sense of stepping above the machinery of his business. For ninety minutes each week, he refused to execute. He refused to respond. He refused to produce.

He observed.

Earlier in his career, which would have felt indulgent. There were always emails to answer, clients to reassure, tasks to complete. Action felt virtuous. Motion felt necessary. But after years of building systems, delegating execution, and refining workflows, Julian recognized something most operators never fully grasp, without altitude, systems decay.

Strategic altitude is not about abstraction for its own sake. It is about upstream correction. It is the discipline of asking why a problem occurred instead of merely fixing what happened.

For a long time, Julian had been excellent at solving visible issues. If a client missed a deadline, they sent reminders. If reporting felt unclear, he clarified the next one. If onboarding stalled, he personally nudged the process forward.

Each fix worked. Each fix also guaranteed recurrence.

Altitude thinking begins when you stop asking how to solve today's problem and start asking why the problem exists structurally.

Julian formalized this habit into a weekly ritual. Every Tuesday, he reviewed the prior seven days not through a lens of accomplishment, but through a lens of friction.

He asked himself what broke. Not catastrophically, but subtly. Where did something require unexpected intervention? Where did a system that should have run smoothly demand manual correction?

He asked what repeated. Which questions did clients ask more than once? Which decisions resurfaced that he believed had already been resolved? Repetition, he learned, was rarely coincidence. It was a signal of incomplete structure.

He asked what drained him disproportionately. Which interactions left him mentally flat for hours? Which tasks required little time but excessive cognitive residue? Energy leaks were often more instructive than revenue reports.

He asked what could be systemized. If something occurred twice in similar form, was it now a candidate for documentation, templating, automation, or delegation?

And finally, he asked what needed elimination. Some tasks did not require refinement; they required removal. Not every recurring activity deserved optimization. Some deserved extinction.

This weekly altitude protocol changed the texture of his growth. Instead of allowing friction to accumulate gradually, he intercepted it early. Minor inefficiencies were resolved before they hardened into habits. Patterns surfaced while still malleable.

Over months, the compounding effect was undeniable. Fewer issues resurfaced. Reactive workload declined. The business felt quieter without becoming stagnant.

But weekly observation alone was insufficient for structural evolution. Every quarter, Julian zoomed out further.

He blocked a full half-day with no operational agenda. He revisited his architecture as if auditing someone else's company. Revenue streams, delivery systems, marketing flows, delegation structures, automation layers—nothing was assumed permanent.

He began by identifying what should be removed. Processes that once served growth but now created drag. Tools that overlapped in functionality. Reports that were generated but rarely used. Removal created immediate clarity.

Next, he examined what could be automated further. Were there still manual transitions between systems? Were reminders dependent on memory? Were repetitive approvals clogging momentum?

Then he evaluated delegation. Had certain decisions remained centralized out of habit rather than necessity? Could authority be redistributed without compromising standards?

After that came reinforcement. Which systems were working well but required strengthening? Did documentation need updating? Did escalation thresholds require clarification? Did monitoring lack depth?

Finally, he considered expansion. With friction reduced and architecture stabilized, where could leverage be extended? New distribution channels. Additional product layers. Improved data visibility.

This quarterly leverage audit prevented drift.

Without cadence, systems degrade quietly. Documentation becomes outdated. Automations misalign with evolving processes. Delegation boundaries blur. Altitude restores intentionality.

The discipline of altitude also changed Julian's emotional relationship with problems. He no longer experienced breakdowns as failures. He experienced them as diagnostic data. A recurring issue was not evidence of incompetence; it was evidence of incomplete architecture.

Upstream problem-solving requires patience because it often demands slower action in the short term. Fixing a broken onboarding manually takes minutes. Redesigning the onboarding system may take hours. But the redesign pays dividends indefinitely.

Earlier in his career, Julian measured progress by how much he accomplished in a day. Now he measured it by how many categories of future work disappeared entirely.

Altitude is not permanent detachment. It is rhythmic elevation. Too much time above the system and you lose proximity to reality. Too little and you become entangled in noise.

The power lies in cadence.

Weekly altitude preserves clarity at the micro level. Quarterly audits preserve integrity at the macro level. Together, they transform leverage from a static build into a living discipline.

By the end of the year, Julian noticed something subtle but profound. Growth no longer felt chaotic. It felt deliberate. Each increase in scale was accompanied by corresponding architectural adjustment. Each new offer integrated into existing systems rather than destabilizing them. Each delegation decision aligned with defined thresholds.

He was no longer reacting to complexity. He was shaping it.

Strategic altitude is the final shift in Part I because it consolidates everything that precedes it. Without altitude, leverage becomes fragile. Without cadence, systems stagnate. Without upstream correction, growth multiplies noise.

But with structured elevation, one person can guide increasingly sophisticated architecture without being consumed by it.

And that is the threshold where operator becomes architect in practice—not as a philosophy, but as a weekly and quarterly habit.

The work continues. But now, it compounds.

PART II, Building the Leverage Stack

Tools, Technology, and Infrastructure for Outsized Output

Every system of intelligent leverage has a spine. A central architecture. A scaffolding that turns scattered tools and ideas into something scalable, sustainable, and effective. In Part I, we examined the mindset shifts that make leverage possible, from operator to architect, from output to infrastructure, from hustle to structure. Now it's time to build the machine.

Part II is where theory becomes execution. It's where scattered actions become systems. We're going to explore the practical side of leverage, the stack you build, layer by layer, to support high-output living as a team of one.

This isn't about being tech-savvy for the sake of it. It's about being leverage-savvy, understanding what tools do for you, when to use them, how to combine them, and how to structure them into workflows that hum quietly in the background while you move forward.

There's a reason most people struggle to scale their time, they jump straight into tools without a solid foundation. They build a Zap here, a rule there, a fancy dashboard that no one uses. And over time, the tool stack becomes more complex than the work it was supposed to simplify. It becomes a liability.

A well-built leverage stack is the opposite of that. It's clean, modular, extensible, and tailored to your work. It adapts as you grow, but it always centers on one goal, to produce more output than your effort would ever allow on its own.

You'll learn how to create systems that move without pushing, respond without prompting, and scale without supervision. You'll understand how to turn emails, notes, files, and forms into structured data you can command. You'll design automations that aren't gimmicks but living logic chains that absorb the burden of your day-to-day operations. You'll discover how to use AI as a collaborator, not just a novelty, and how to visualize everything through a central dashboard that makes complexity manageable.

Most importantly, you'll begin to experience a shift in your role. The stack doesn't just free up time. It elevates your thinking. It creates enough margin to finally solve the problems you've been too busy to fix. And that's where the real compound returns begin.

So, let's move from mindset to mechanics. Let's build the backbone of your invisible team.

Chapter 11, The Stack Is the Business

When Daniel first began consulting independently, he believed that growth was a function of reputation and skill. If he became better at delivering insight, clearer in communication, and more persuasive in sales conversations, the business would naturally expand. For several years that assumption held. Revenue increased steadily. Referrals arrived. Demand seemed to correlate directly with competence.

The first inflection point disrupted that belief. Revenue rose sharply within a single quarter without a corresponding increase in hours worked. He did not meaningfully change his offer. He did not significantly increase marketing output. Yet the business handled more volume with less strain.

The explanation, which only became obvious in hindsight, was structural maturation.

Up until that period, Daniel's company functioned as an extension of his working memory. Every transition depended on him noticing it. When a prospect sent an inquiry, he manually categorized it. When a contract was signed, he manually initiated onboarding steps. When payment arrived, he manually confirmed activation. When projects advanced, he manually adjusted timelines. Each step required awareness, and awareness required attention.

Attention is not a scalable resource.

The redesign began accidentally. After missing an onboarding step for a new client—an oversight caused by overlapping conversations—Daniel decided to formalize the activation phase of his client lifecycle. Instead of initiating onboarding via a loose email thread, he created a structured intake confirmation that triggered a predefined sequence. That sequence assembled documentation, provisioned a shared workspace, issued billing instructions, and created internal project milestones automatically.

The immediate effect was modest, fewer errors and less mental overhead. The cumulative effect was substantial, activation no longer required supervision.

That moment prompted a broader question. If activation could be structured, what about every other transition?

He began mapping the lifecycle of his business not by services delivered, but by state changes. A prospect becomes a qualified lead. A qualified lead becomes a signed client. A signed client becomes an active project. An active project becomes a completed engagement. A completed engagement becomes either a referral source or a dormant record.

Each of those transitions required information movement, decision logic, and confirmation.

Previously, those movements were implicit. They happened because Daniel noticed them and acted. Now he began externalizing them.

The capture layer was redesigned first. Every meaningful external interaction had to produce structured data rather than free-form communication. Inquiry forms were standardized to gather relevant context before conversation. Discovery calls were summarized using predefined fields. Proposals were generated from modular components tied to specific service types.

This shift alone reduced ambiguity. But the real leverage emerged in the processing layer.

Instead of copying data between systems manually, Daniel connected state changes to triggers. When a proposal status changed to approved, a contract generation sequence began automatically. When a contract was executed, onboarding was initiated without additional intervention. When onboarding was completed, billing was activated according to predefined schedules. When payment cleared, the project board unlocked milestone tasks.

The stack had begun to carry transitions.

As volume increased, the importance of integration became clearer. A business with five clients can tolerate loosely connected tools. A business with fifty cannot. Disconnected platforms create invisible friction because data must be reconciled manually. Each reconciliation consumes cognitive energy and introduces risk.

Daniel gradually consolidated systems around a single source of truth for client status. Every other component referenced that central record. Reporting dashboards pulled directly from it. Task boards updated automatically when status fields changed.

Communication sequences referenced stored metadata instead of requiring manual segmentation.

The stack now resembled a coordinated architecture rather than a set of utilities.

At this point, Daniel began distinguishing between tools and structure. A tool performs a function. Structure determines how functions interact. A calendar tool schedules meetings. A structured stack ensures that meetings, once scheduled, trigger preparation workflows, follow-up reminders, and documentation storage without manual prompting.

The insight that reshaped his thinking was simple but consequential, the business was not his expertise. The business was the stack that moved expertise through defined channels.

Expertise attracted demand. The stack determined capacity.

This distinction became most visible during an unexpected test. Daniel was forced to step away for two weeks due to a family emergency. In earlier years, that absence would have destabilized operations. Instead, the system absorbed most of the impact. Client onboarding continued. Billing cycles executed. Reporting was generated. Minor questions escalated according to predefined rules. Upon return, the backlog was manageable rather than catastrophic.

The stack had achieved a degree of autonomy.

Autonomy, however, does not arise from automation alone. It requires clarity in three dimensions, data structure, transition logic, and oversight.

Data structure ensures that information enters in predictable formats. Transition logic defines what happens when states change. Oversight provides visibility into system health.

Daniel formalized oversight through dashboards that surfaced only relevant metrics. He did not attempt to monitor everything. Instead, he defined key performance indicators tied directly to structural health, onboarding completion time, billing accuracy rate, project milestone adherence, response latency thresholds. Deviations triggered alerts rather than passive observation.

At this stage, artificial intelligence began playing a supporting role. Rather than using AI as a generic writing assistant, Daniel embedded it into defined workflows. After discovery calls, transcripts were processed through structured prompts that extracted goals, constraints, and objections into standardized fields. Proposal drafts were generated from these structured summaries, reducing preparation time while maintaining strategic coherence. Recurring client questions were analyzed quarterly to identify pattern gaps in onboarding documentation.

AI did not replace decision-making. It accelerated structured processing.

Over time, the stack evolved from a pipeline into a feedback-driven system. Outputs generated data that informed refinement. If onboarding confusion increased, documentation was updated.

If proposals required excessive revision, templates were refined. If client retention dipped, milestone pacing was reassessed.

The stack became self-correcting because it produced visibility.

With visibility came discipline. Daniel discovered that growth did not require adding layers indefinitely. Each addition had to strengthen coherence. When new tools introduced duplication or required excessive maintenance, they were removed. When integrations created fragility, they were simplified.

The most difficult lesson was restraint. It is tempting to overbuild once structural leverage becomes visible. But complexity compounds just as power does. A stack must feel lighter as it scales, not heavier.

By the end of the year, Daniel understood that what he had built was not simply efficiency. He had separated production from supervision. The system produced reliably. He supervised strategically.

That separation is the threshold where a business stops being an extension of personal labor and becomes an engineered environment.

The stack, properly designed, is not background infrastructure.

It is the business itself.

Chapter 12, Beginner and Advanced Stack Architectures

When Lena started her advisory firm, she believed that sophistication was a future problem. Her immediate goal was stability. She wanted consistent clients, clean delivery, and enough revenue to justify leaving her corporate role permanently. Because she had watched other founders drown in software before earning meaningful income, she intentionally kept her toolset minimal. A calendar application, a shared document platform, a basic invoicing system, and email. Nothing more.

For the first few months, this restraint felt wise. There were few clients. Transitions between stages were manageable. If a prospect emailed her directly, she responded. If someone agreed to work together, they manually sent a welcome packet she had saved in a folder. She created a shared workspace from a copied template and drafted invoices individually. None of these actions consumed extraordinary time.

The friction did not appear as overload. It appeared as mental fragmentation.

Each client existed in a slightly different state, tracked in slightly different places. Some details lived in email threads. Others in a spreadsheet she updated inconsistently. A few notes remained in her head because documenting them felt unnecessary. Nothing was broken, but nothing was structurally coherent.

The first true strain emerged when three new clients signed within the same week. The workload itself was not unmanageable, but the coordination exposed weakness. She sent two slightly different versions of onboarding instructions because she edited them manually each time. She forgot to create one shared folder until the client asked where to upload files. She nearly delayed an invoice because payment terms were not embedded anywhere except in a past email thread.

That week forced her to see something clearly, the business did not need more tools. It needed fewer transitions that depended on memory.

The redesign began not with software selection but with lifecycle mapping. She sat down and described, in writing, what actually happens when someone moves from stranger to completed client. She did not describe services or value propositions. She described state changes. A stranger becomes an inquirer. An inquirer becomes a scheduled conversation. A scheduled conversation becomes either disqualified or proposed. A proposal becomes accepted. An accepted proposal becomes active engagement. An engagement becomes completed work.

When she wrote those transitions down in full sentences, she noticed that every change of state required her intervention. There were no triggers embedded in the system itself. Nothing happened unless she initiated it consciously.

The beginner stack is not defined by tool simplicity; it is defined by transition reliability. At Lena's stage, complexity would have introduced maintenance overhead without proportional benefit. What she needed was structural coherence.

She chose a single system to act as the authoritative record of client status. Every prospect, regardless of how they arrived, had to exist in that central location. If someone emailed her directly, she entered them manually rather than allowing information to live in fragmented threads. When she changed a prospect's status to "proposal accepted," that status change became the single initiating event for onboarding. Instead of sending a welcome email manually, she built a predefined sequence tied to that state change. The welcome packet was standardized. The shared workspace was generated from a master structure she refined deliberately. The invoice was scheduled automatically according to stored payment terms.

The architecture was simple, but the shift was profound. She was no longer performing onboarding. She was supervising onboarding.

This distinction matters because supervision scales more easily than execution. A beginner stack should remove ambiguity and prevent omission. It should not attempt to anticipate behavioral segmentation or advanced analytics. Its purpose is to eliminate the founder as the bridge between recurring states.

Victor's business existed on a different terrain. By the time Daniel began advising him, Victor managed multiple revenue streams. He operated a subscription community, cohort-based programs, and advisory retainers. Thousands of subscribers entered his ecosystem through varied channels, podcast interviews, paid advertisements, referrals, organic search.

Unlike Lena's linear lifecycle, Victor's environment was multi-directional. A subscriber might begin with free content, purchase a low-ticket product, upgrade to a cohort program, pause for several months, then reengage through a live event. Each interaction produced behavioral data that, if ignored, reduced strategic clarity.

Victor initially tried to manage this complexity manually. He reviewed spreadsheets to track purchases. He skimmed email analytics to assess engagement. He relied on intuition to determine which segment of his audience to address next. As volume increased, intuition became unreliable. Important signals were buried in noise.

The advanced stack does not primarily solve transition reliability; it solves information coherence under scale.

Daniel guided Victor through reconstructing his architecture around layered integration. Instead of allowing each platform to operate independently, Victor identified a central data model that defined what a "customer" actually meant in his ecosystem. This model included fields for engagement history, purchase record, participation status, and behavioral indicators.

Every external interaction had to update that record automatically. When someone attended a live session, the attendance was logged structurally. When a subscriber clicked through three consecutive emails on a specific topic, that pattern was recorded. When a member completed a course module, progress status updated their profile.

These updates were not collected for vanity metrics. They informed decision logic. If a customer demonstrated consistent engagement with leadership content, invitations to advanced programs reflected that interest. If a subscriber purchased a product but never activated access, a follow-up sequence addressed onboarding friction rather than promoting new offers.

The advanced stack introduces adaptive logic. It recognizes that not all participants move linearly. It encodes decision trees based on behavior rather than static segmentation.

However, Daniel insisted on one governing principle, complexity must serve clarity. Victor was tempted to introduce elaborate automation sequences for rare edge cases. Daniel required justification. If a process occurred infrequently, manual handling remained preferable. Advanced architecture should reduce founder cognitive load, not increase system maintenance.

The contrast between Lena and Victor illustrates the true difference between beginner and advanced stacks. The beginner stack protects against instability by structuring predictable transitions. The advanced stack manages complexity by structuring data relationships and behavioral logic.

Both require discipline. Both require restraint. Both demand that tools serve architecture rather than dictate it.

When founders misunderstand maturity, they either attempt advanced segmentation before achieving basic reliability, or they resist integration long after complexity demands it. The art lies in matching architecture to current constraint, not aspirational identity.

A stack is not impressive because it is sophisticated. It is effective because it aligns structure with stage.

Chapter 13, AI as a Structured Processing Layer

When Victor first integrated artificial intelligence into his stack, he treated it like a creative assistant. He would open a blank interface, type a loosely formed request, and evaluate whatever came back. Some outputs were useful. Others required significant revision. The variability made it unreliable, and unreliability made it difficult to embed into real operations.

The shift occurred when he stopped thinking of AI as a conversational partner and began treating it as a deterministic processing layer.

In his business, the most time-consuming cognitive bottleneck was synthesis. Discovery calls generated unstructured insight. Customer support emails contained patterns that were not immediately visible. Survey responses accumulated faster than he could interpret them. The work was not mechanical; it was analytical. Yet much of the analysis followed repeatable logic.

He began with discovery calls.

Previously, after each call, he would re-listen to sections of the recording and manually extract objectives, constraints, decision drivers, and timeline pressures. The quality of his proposals depended heavily on how well he structured this information. The thinking itself was consistent across clients. What varied were the details.

Instead of drafting proposals from scratch, he redesigned the process. Every call was recorded and transcribed automatically. The transcript was passed into a structured prompt template that specified role, output format, evaluation criteria, and extraction fields. The prompt did not ask for a "summary." It required defined sections, stated goals, unstated goals inferred from tone, explicit constraints, implicit risks, timeline sensitivity, budget indicators, and potential objections.

Because the input was standardized and the extraction logic was fixed, the output became predictable. He then fed that structured extraction into a modular proposal generator that assembled sections dynamically. If a timeline constraint was tight, the implementation roadmap adjusted automatically. If budget sensitivity was detected, optional phased deliverables were included.

AI did not replace strategic judgment. It accelerated structured organization.

He applied similar logic to customer feedback. Thousands of support messages had accumulated across channels. Reading them individually was inefficient but ignoring them left blind spots. Instead of manually sampling messages, he exported them into categorized batches. Each batch was processed through a structured analytical prompt that required classification into friction categories, frequency estimation, emotional intensity markers, and suggested root causes.

Patterns emerged that were previously invisible. A significant portion of churn was linked not to product quality, but to onboarding confusion in the first seven days. That insight prompted structural redesign of activation flow rather than surface-level content updates.

The key realization was that AI functions best when embedded inside clearly defined inputs and outputs. When treated casually, it produces variable creativity. When treated architecturally, it produces reliable processing.

Victor built a version-controlled prompt library. Each prompt template was documented with purpose, expected input format, output structure, and revision history. If a refinement improved clarity or reduced hallucination risk, it was saved as a new version rather than overwritten. Over time, this library became an internal toolkit. He was no longer improvising interactions. He was deploying predefined capabilities.

He also learned where not to insert AI. Negotiation emails requiring tone sensitivity remained manually written. High-stakes strategic pivots were never automated. The discipline lay in identifying repeatable cognitive labor, not creative authorship.

Once embedded properly, AI reduces what Victor began to think of as analysis drag. Raw information no longer lingered in unstructured form. Transcripts, feedback, surveys, and performance metrics entered the system as inputs and emerged as organized insight. His role shifted upward. He was no longer spending hours parsing and synthesizing. He was evaluating, refining, and directing.

The transformation, however, revealed something important. Intelligence alone does not create scale. Structured prompts and refined outputs improved clarity, but they still depended on how information moved through the broader system. If transcripts were not routed correctly, if feedback was not centralized, if data remained scattered across tools, the processing layer had nothing reliable to work with. AI could accelerate thinking, but it could not compensate for fragmented infrastructure.

At that point, the limitation was no longer cognitive. It was architectural. The more capable the processing layer became, the more obvious the weaknesses of the underlying backbone appeared. Insight required clean inputs. Clean inputs required connectivity. Connectivity required deliberate design. If AI was the analytical engine, something else had to function as the nervous system that carried signals between every part of the operation. Without that backbone, intelligence remained powerful but isolated.

The next stage was no longer about prompting better. It was about building a digital spine strong enough to support everything that intelligence made possible.

Chapter 14, Infrastructure of One

Your digital backbone, APIs, dashboards, and cloud intelligence

There is a moment in every solo operator's journey when the cracks begin to show. The surface may still look polished, clients are happy, invoices are going out, and content is being published, but behind the scenes, the wheels are coming off.. Files are scattered. Tasks are tracked across five different platforms. Notes live in Slack messages and half-finished Google Docs. Updates are manual. Nothing talks to anything else. And worst of all, everything depends on memory.

At this point, most people try to work harder. They promise to be more organized, more disciplined, more vigilant. They buy a new app or hire a virtual assistant to keep up. But the real solution isn't better habits. It has better *infrastructure.*

Every business, whether it has one person or one hundred, runs on infrastructure. The only difference is visibility. In a traditional organization, there are departments, servers, IT teams, and org charts. In a solo operation, it's easy to pretend you don't need those things until you do.

The Infrastructure of one is what separates the chaotic freelancer from the architected entrepreneur. It's the quiet, under-the-hood system that holds your entire digital ecosystem together. It's the APIs that move data without you. It's the dashboards that make complexity visible. It's the smart folders, auto-tagging, and logic flows that let you run a complex business without feeling like one.

When people say they want to scale, what they often mean is they want their work to grow without breaking. And that means building a spine strong enough to support it. Infrastructure isn't sexy. It doesn't get likes. But it's what allows everything else to move with grace.

At the heart of this is connectivity. The best solo operators understand that their tools can't live in silos. They build an environment where their calendar integrates with their CRM, their forms connect to their databases, and their content libraries are fed into their publishing systems. Nothing gets copied and pasted manually. Nothing gets double-entered. The system handles the handoff.

That connectivity often starts with APIs, the invisible pipelines that let different platforms share information. You don't need to be a developer to use them. Platforms like Zapier, Make, and Pipedream let you build those bridges without writing a line of code. You set the rules, and the system moves the data. The result isn't just saved time, it's reduced friction, improved consistency, and a system that scales itself.

Imagine someone books a call on your site. Instantly, their info is added to your CRM, their time zone is noted, a prep form is sent, a Slack message goes out, a task is created to review their file, and a thank-you email is scheduled post-call. All of this happens in under ten seconds, without you touching anything.

That's not productivity. That's *infrastructure.*

But automation without visibility is dangerous. This is where dashboards come in. Your infrastructure should tell you what it's doing. It should surface the correct information at the right time, your pipeline, your weekly metrics, your open tasks, and your client statuses. It should reduce the need to "check in" or "remember." A good dashboard replaces anxiety with clarity.

And dashboards don't need to be complex. A Notion database with filtered views. A Google Sheet with innovative formulas. A Trello board that visualizes stages. What matters is that your information isn't buried. It's *framed.* You're not digging for data; you're scanning for insight.

The Infrastructure of One is also about storage and retrieval. If you've ever spent ten minutes searching for a file you know exists, you've felt the pain of disorganized knowledge. Excellent infrastructure eliminates that. It gives every piece of data a home and a logic for getting there. Your assets are tagged. Your notes are linked. Your client files follow a naming convention. Your documentation lives where you expect it to. You don't *search,* you retrieve.

And when retrieval is instant, your mental load drops. You're no longer carrying the burden of where things are, what's due, or who said what. Your system remembers for you. You become a better thinker because you're no longer a full-time memory manager.

One of the most underappreciated benefits of digital infrastructure is how it frees your attention. The brain wasn't designed to track workflows, deadlines, filenames, and follow-ups. When all of that is outsourced to a reliable, visible system, your cognitive resources are finally available for higher-level work, strategy, writing, vision, and decision-making.

This is where cloud intelligence comes into play. More than just where things are stored, the cloud becomes your *operational nervous system*. It's not just about access; it's about real-time awareness. Your tools are always on. Your files are always synced. Your AI assistants always have the context. And your entire digital environment is accessible from anywhere, structured to function without your real-time oversight.

And as AI continues to evolve, your infrastructure will only get smarter. Your automations won't just be rule-based; they'll be adaptive. Your dashboards will show insights, not just data. Your file systems will suggest what you need next. The Infrastructure of One becomes increasingly self-aware. It doesn't just reflect your work; it *extends* your capacity.

But all of this begins with intention. The operators who build strong infrastructure do so before they need it. They don't wait for the wheels to fall off. They recognize that every system they rely on, whether for communication, task management, or delivery, needs to be *designed*, not just assembled.

They stop using tools reactively. They begin building an environment in which the tools serve the system, and the system serves the mission.

When your infrastructure is strong, you don't fear growth. You don't dread taking on more. You don't waste energy worrying about what will fall through the cracks. You *trust the machine*. You know what it can handle. And you know how to improve it.

This is the freedom most solopreneurs never taste. Not because it's inaccessible, but because infrastructure feels like overhead. It's not. Its *capacity*. It's the foundation on which a sustainable scale is built.

Because in the end, the difference between a stressed-out operator and a clear-minded builder isn't talent. It's what's behind the scenes.

And the solo business that looks effortless on the surface always rests on invisible infrastructure that was carefully designed, line by line, connection by connection, insight by insight.

Chapter 15, No-Code as Your Operations Department

Replacing manual work with modular, drag-and-drop systems.

There was a time when building systems meant writing code. You had to understand syntax, logic trees, error handling, and server environments. If you weren't technical, your ideas had to pass through a developer or die on your whiteboard. That bottleneck left countless systems unbuilt, workflows unscaled, and problems unsolved. But then something changed. Quietly, steadily, the barrier dropped. And with it, a revolution began.

No-code tools have turned non-developers into system architects. What once took a software engineer three weeks can now be accomplished in an afternoon by someone who doesn't know a line of JavaScript. Drag, drop, connect. Build, test, refine. The result? What was once expensive, slow, and inaccessible is now just a browser tab away.

No-code is not just a trend. It's a foundational shift in how operations get built. It's the toolkit of the modern solo operator who refuses to be limited by technical skills. And when treated with intention, no-code becomes your silent operations department, handling everything from onboarding and fulfillment to marketing, scheduling, data routing, and reporting.

But to truly leverage no-code, you need to approach it with more than curiosity. You need to treat it like *infrastructure design*. The tools are easy to use, but the architecture still matters.

Operators who treat no-code as a toy end up with half-finished workflows and brittle automations. Operators who treat no-code as *infrastructure* build businesses that hum along quietly, scaling up or down without chaos.

The first step is understanding that no-code isn't one tool, it's an ecosystem. Each platform does one thing exceptionally well. Airtable acts as your relational database, giving structure to your backend without writing SQL. Zapier or Make serves as connective tissue, moving data and triggering workflows. Notion or Coda can serve as your documentation hubs, dashboards, or even lightweight CRMs. Webflow can build your public-facing presence. Tally or Typeform gathers structured input. The magic happens when these pieces talk to each other.

Imagine this, a lead fills out a form on your site. That data is routed to Airtable, which instantly categorizes the lead by priority. A record is created in your CRM view, a welcome email is triggered, and a Slack message pings you with context. The client is sent a proposal via a templated tool like Better Proposals or PandaDoc. If they sign, the workflow continues, the invoice is created, the onboarding form is sent, and the scheduling link is dispatched. You didn't touch a thing. But your business moved forward.

That's no-code functioning not as a gimmick, but as *operations*.

What makes this so powerful isn't just that it saves time. It replaces the constant switching, checking, reminding, and nudging that most businesses rely on. It gives your work *continuity.* You don't need to remember where a lead is in the pipeline. The system already knows. You don't need to chase documents or status updates. They're already logged and visible.

This kind of continuity is what turns chaos into clarity. And clarity, more than anything else, is what preserves your attention for the work that matters.

No-code also introduces a new kind of agility. In a traditional business, changing a process means a new dev ticket, a new round of testing, and another sprint. In a no-code business, you open the visual editor, adjust a field, update the automation, and move on. The time between idea and execution shrinks dramatically. This allows you to *respond to your business in real time,* to experiment, iterate, and evolve without getting bogged down.

It also means that your systems grow with you. You don't need to build the enterprise version on day one. You can start with a single form and a two-step automation. As complexity increases, you modularize. You layer in conditions, approvals, dashboards, and integrations. But because you built it yourself, or at least understood how it was built, you're never at the mercy of someone else's roadmap.

And that autonomy is worth its weight in gold.

But for all its advantages, no-code does require discipline. Because it's easy, it's tempting to overbuild. To create clever automations that nobody uses. To chase novelty instead of solving problems. This is where the systems-first mindset becomes critical. Every tool you use should earn its place. Every workflow should map to a transparent, repeatable process. You're not building for fun. You're building for function.

Documentation is your safeguard. As your no-code operations grow, you need a source of truth. How does this workflow operate? What triggers it? Where is the data stored? What happens if it fails? When you embed this thinking into your operations, you create *resilience.* Your systems can be paused, audited, handed off, and restarted without mystery.

The best no-code businesses are often invisible. They don't look flashy. They work—clean data, clear handoffs, timely communication, consistent outcomes. To the outside world, it feels like magic. But you know what's under the hood, well-designed systems made possible by a stack of simple, interoperable tools.

And increasingly, these tools are integrating with AI. You can have a GPT agent trigger inside a Make scenario to summarize data, write personalized copy, or make decisions based on logic you define. You can connect sentiment analysis to customer feedback, train chatbots on your SOPs, or route requests through AI triage systems. What you're building isn't just automation, it's a responsive, intelligent backend.

This is what it means to have no-code as your operations department. Your technical skills, your team size, or your bandwidth no longer limit you. You've built a digital workforce that handles the weight of delivery, tracking, routing, and follow-up, leaving you with clarity, capacity, and freedom.

The real win isn't the saved time. It's the *elevated role*. You become the designer of systems that grow, not the manager of tasks that repeat.

And in that role, you discover something powerful, scale isn't about doing more. It's about *doing less of the right things with better systems behind you.*

No-code gave you the keys. It's time to drive like someone who's building a company, not just running a calendar.

Chapter 16, AI as a Thought Partner

From prompt engineering to decision-making augmentation

For decades, artificial intelligence lived in the realm of speculation. It was the stuff of sci-fi novels and futurist conferences, impressive in theory, mysterious in practice. But over the last few years, AI has quietly stepped out of the abstract and into our workflows, not as a looming replacement, but as something more useful, more practical, and ultimately, more powerful, a thought partner.

This is the form of AI that belongs in your leverage stack. Not a robotic overlord or a black-box oracle, but a responsive, tireless collaborator. A system that helps you think faster, decide smarter, and create more freely. A partner that never gets tired, never loses focus, and never asks for credit.

When people think about using AI, they often imagine task automation, having GPT draft an email, summarize a meeting, or spit out some quick content. And yes, those use cases matter. But the fundamental shift begins when you stop using AI as a tool and start working with it as an *extension of your cognition.*

The leverage isn't in speed alone. It's in scale. It's in how much mental effort you can now outsource, not just in execution, but in ideation, planning, refinement, and simulation.

Imagine you're writing a product launch sequence. Instead of starting from nothing, you ask your AI to list five angles based on your last campaign. Then you request an outline for each. You explore tone options, reorder the structure, and stress test the copy. The AI responds instantly, adapting to your inputs, surfacing blind spots, and suggesting alternatives. You're not just using a writing tool. You're collaborating with something that holds context, asks the right questions, and never needs a break.

This is what it means to treat AI as a thought partner. You don't just tell it what to do. You *work together*, each of you iterating, refining, and shaping the output.

But for this partnership to be effective, you need to learn a new language, the language of *prompt architecture*. A prompt isn't just a command. It's a form of programming. The way you frame your request, the context you provide, the format you ask for, and the constraints you add will determine the quality of the result. Garbage in, garbage out isn't just a cliché. It's the governing rule of generative systems.

The best operators know this. They don't type in vague questions and hope for brilliance. They build prompt templates. They feed in samples. They train their models on their voice, thinking patterns, and decision logic. Over time, the AI evolves from a generic assistant into a personal strategy layer, reflecting your mental models to you with speed and scale.

And the partnership deepens.

You use AI to generate naming options, then to critique them. You have to synthesize customer feedback and highlight themes. You feed it transcripts from coaching calls or sales meetings and ask it to extract signals, concerns, and language patterns. You build internal agents that handle specific thinking tasks, voice assistants, content strategists, and outreach analyzers, all trained on your frameworks.

It's not just about reducing work. It's about enhancing the *quality* of thinking. You no longer sit in a room alone, staring at the ceiling, hoping insight strikes. You begin every important thinking session with an AI prompt, not for the answer, but for momentum. And from there, the collaboration begins.

This matters because the actual cost of high-leverage work is *cognitive load*. Big decisions require energy. Creativity requires fuel. Context-switching between dozens of micro-decisions throughout the day erodes your ability to focus on what moves the needle. AI, when used well, becomes your buffer. It holds the smaller weights so you can lift the big ones.

You might still make the final call. But AI can lay out the options, test the assumptions, and even generate the counterarguments. That's not artificial intelligence replacing human judgment; it's augmenting it.

This becomes even more valuable when you're building systems. You can use AI to write SOPs, improve documentation, suggest automation sequences, test customer personas, or refine onboarding flows. You can ask it to compare tools based on your specific needs. You can even simulate how a new process might fail and use the result to add preventative structure.

In short, AI becomes your *simulation engine*.

Every great strategist understands the value of running scenarios. But most don't have time to do it well. Now, with a prompt and a model trained on your domain, you can play out possibilities at high speed. You can see what a plan looks like if it succeeds, and what it looks like if it breaks. That insight alone can save months of frustration.

And here's where the partnership truly shifts, AI becomes part of your leverage loop.

You build systems. Those systems generate data. You feed that data back into your AI tools. Your tools surface insights. You make better decisions. Those decisions improve your systems. And the loop accelerates.

This loop doesn't require a team. It doesn't require a budget. It involves *design*, the willingness to treat AI not as a trick, but as a teammate.

That also means building guardrails. AI can hallucinate. It can misread nuance. It can produce generic fluff if left unsupervised. That's why your role remains essential, not as the one doing all the work, but as the one *guiding the quality of thinking*. You're still the strategist. The model is your amplifier.

Over time, you'll develop AI workflows as naturally as you create email templates or process maps. You'll start your day not with a to-do list, but with a collaboration list, things your AI agent can work on while you focus elsewhere. You'll learn which prompts produce insight, which make noise, and how to refine the difference.

Eventually, the line between human and system will blur, not in a dystopian sense, but in an efficient one. You'll move faster because you're no longer moving alone.

That's what it means to use AI as a thought partner. It's not about replacing your brain. It's about expanding your reach.

Because the future doesn't belong to the person who knows the most.

It belongs to the person who builds the most competent partner and knows how to think with it.

Chapter 17, Capture and Command, Mastering Your Input Layer

How to control emails, notes, ideas, and content streams with minimal effort

There is a moment, often unnoticed, when a high-leverage day begins to fall apart. It's not dramatic. It doesn't announce itself. But somewhere between the third email, the half-formed idea, and the Slack ping that drags you sideways, the clarity slips. And what takes its place is noise, scattered, incoming, relentless. If you're not careful, your entire day becomes a reaction to unfiltered inputs.

Most people think their problem is distraction. But in reality, their problem is *capture* Or rather, the lack of it. Ideas float by and are lost. Tasks arise and vanish. Notes are jotted down in five different places. Emails arrive without structure, messages pile up, and bookmarks go forgotten. The brain tries to hold it all and predictably fails. And then, at 10,47 p.m., you remember the thing you were supposed to do this morning. Too late. Again.

This is not a discipline issue. It's a systems issue. And the solution begins with a radical idea, you should never be the primary storage unit for your own life. Your brain is not designed to hold information. It's designed to *make decisions with it.* The key is creating an input layer that reliably catches everything you care about and routes it to the right place without demanding your constant attention.

The input layer is the quiet foundation of any leverage system. It's the inbox behind the scenes, not just your email inbox, but the collective set of channels where tasks, ideas, requests, and opportunities enter your world. It includes your actual inbox, yes, but also your calendar, your voice notes, your form submissions, your Slack messages, your DMs, your content feeds, your note-taking apps, your reminders, and your internal thoughts.

The goal isn't to eliminate these channels. The goal is to centralize their flow. To create a structure where all inputs, regardless of where they start, end up somewhere *capturable, reviewable, and actionable.*

Imagine a system where emails are auto-categorized, messages tagged by sender type, voice notes transcribed and routed to your notes database, incoming ideas logged with context, forms sorted by urgency, and all of it visible from a central dashboard. This isn't fantasy. This is what happens when you build a deliberate input layer.

You begin by identifying your sources. Where does information come in? How often? What kind of inputs do they represent? What do you *want* to keep, and what should be blocked at the gate?

For most people, email is the primary culprit. It's not just the volume. The issue lies in email being treated as both a communication tool and a task manager, roles it was never intended to fulfill. A leveraged operator separates those layers. They route important emails to task systems or CRMs. They snooze or archive messages that don't require action. They use auto-filters, rules, and labels to sort before reading. And most importantly, they stop using the inbox as a to-do list.

The same principle applies to every other channel. DMs shouldn't be where projects live. Slack shouldn't be your archive of client decisions. Meeting notes shouldn't be trapped in random files. Every input needs a *next step*. It's either stored, actioned, delegated, scheduled, or deleted.

This is where tools like Notion, Obsidian, Roam, or Tana become critical. They act as your second brain, your digital catcher's mitt. But the tools themselves aren't the solution. The *flow* is. What matters is that every thought, task, note, or request enters a system where it can be retrieved and acted upon. Without this, every other layer of leverage collapses. You can't automate chaos. You can only scale it.

The capture system needs to be fast, frictionless, and omnipresent. That means being able to log an idea from your phone in three seconds. It means being able to forward an email to your task system with one click. It means dictating a thought while walking and knowing it will land in the right inbox. You don't wait until you have time to organize. You build a system that *collects as you go*.

One robust frame is to think of your input layer like a logistics hub. Information comes in from multiple locations. The hub doesn't *do* the work; it just sorts and dispatches it. Urgent items are routed to action lists. Research items go to long-term memory. Meeting outcomes are logged in CRM fields. Raw ideas go into a project notebook for later review. And nothing sits untagged, unlabeled, or invisible.

The result is clarity. Not because there's less information, but because *you know where it all lives*. You don't have to remember what that client said last week. You don't have to search fifteen channels to find the note you made at the gym. You know it's in the system, and the system is searchable.

Just as important, the system *protects your attention*. You're no longer reacting in real-time to every incoming input. You've created buffers, rules, automations, and inboxes that separate the moment of arrival from the moment of processing. You check when *you're ready*, not when the internet wants your attention.

This creates space not just in your calendar, but in your mind. You begin to think proactively again. You regain the ability to do deep work, confident that nothing urgent is being forgotten, and that everything non-urgent is being captured.

That's the paradox of leverage, the more input you can handle without stress, the more output you can create with intention. Most people get overwhelmed by input because they try to hold it all mentally. The leveraged operator captures *everything* and holds on to *nothing*. The system does the remembering. You do the deciding.

Eventually, this becomes second nature. You hear a good idea and instinctively log it. You get a task by text and know exactly how to route it. You read a comment thread and extract the one insight worth saving. The world becomes signal-rich because your filter is strong.

And at scale, the system begins to think with you. AI tools can begin tagging content automatically, suggesting links between notes, or surfacing related ideas at just the right time. You're not just capturing. You're *commanding* a flow of information that works with you, not against you.

The goal isn't perfection. Its reliability. And once your input layer is reliable, the rest of your leverage stack can stand on solid ground.

Because the real power isn't just in knowing what to do, it's in *always knowing where to find it.*

Chapter 18, Output Architecture

Designing content, product, and asset systems that scale without you.

Most people think of output as the final step, something you produce once a decision has been made or a project has been completed. But in a high-leverage system, output isn't a last-minute scramble. It's a design layer. A structured, repeatable process for turning ideas into artifacts, systems into assets, and knowledge into results that don't rely on your real-time presence.

This is the essence of output architecture, designing your business and creative systems to produce with consistency, without bottlenecks in your daily effort. It's the shift from *creating on demand* to *building outputs on rails,* systems that generate value with minimal input and maximum reuse.

Most operators are so focused on getting things done that they never step back to ask, *How does my work become repeatable?* How does it scale beyond me? How do I create something once and deploy it multiple times? Without an output architecture, you're trapped in a loop of endless doing. With it, your work becomes a machine, structured, leveraged, and extensible.

Let's take content as an example. A single podcast episode, article, or client email can become a cascade of outputs, quotes, social posts, newsletter entries, video clips, course modules, even future product ideas. But only if you *design for it* from the start. If your content system doesn't capture context, isolate components, or feed into a broader pipeline, then each piece becomes a one-off. Valuable once, forgotten forever.

The leveraged creator builds differently. They tag content by topic, audience, and format. They extract key ideas into a database. They use AI tools to spin variations, test angles, and repackage for different platforms. They connect input to output so that one good piece of thinking never stops working.

This principle extends far beyond content. Client deliverables, internal documentation, proposals, templates, designs —anything you produce more than once — is a candidate for architecture. The key is to stop treating outputs as *events* and start treating them as *systems.*

Ask yourself, What do I produce more than twice? Where am I reinventing the wheel? What deliverables could become products? What notes could become assets? What decisions could become frameworks?

The goal isn't to mechanize creativity. It's to *support* it. The more structure you build into your output layer, the more creative energy you free up. You're not designing the ideas. You're creating the flow. That flow becomes the architecture, channels, templates, logic, and timelines that ensure your thinking becomes action and your action becomes assets.

One of the most powerful unlocks here is template-first thinking. If you build a proposal once, that's fine. If you use it again without modification, that's useful. But if you extract the structure, introduction, pain points, solution layout, deliverables, call to action, and turn it into a dynamic template that adapts to different clients, that's architecture.

Templates aren't about laziness. They're about *intention.* A well-built template doesn't just save time; it improves consistency, elevates quality, and removes decision fatigue. It ensures that every version of an output meets your standard, even when you're not the one producing it.

Another piece of output architecture is the production pipeline. This is the engine that moves work from idea to execution to publication or delivery. In a leveraged system, this pipeline is visible, predictable, and team-proof. Whether it's content, client work, or product development, the process follows a structured path, intake, draft, review, optimize, publish. Each stage has an owner, a checklist, and a deadline.

But most importantly, the system runs *without your real-time input.* You may still oversee it. But you're not the one moving the files, sending the emails, or checking the formatting. The architecture holds that. It ensures outputs are produced on time, to spec, with minimal stress.

At its highest level, output architecture supports compound leverage. This is where your outputs *produce other outputs.* A keynote talk becomes a YouTube series. A tweetstorm becomes a guide. A client framework becomes a course. A recurring insight becomes a product. This flywheel doesn't happen by accident. It's the result of systems built for reuse, remixing, and redistribution.

AI supercharges this even further. You can now take a transcript and ask your AI to turn it into five blog posts, three quote cards, two emails, and a lead magnet. You can feed raw data into a model and have it generate insights, visuals, or summaries. But again, the key isn't the AI. It's the *system around it* that captures, tags, filters, and routes those outputs where they need to go.

That's output architecture, the deliberate design of a world in which your best thinking is captured, your best work is amplified, and your best systems are never lost to a forgotten file or a misnamed folder.

Even something as simple as file naming becomes a leverage point. Do you label your assets with client, date, and version? Are they searchable? Are they stored in a way that a new team member can find and use them instantly? Architecture isn't just about tools. It's about *decisions that prevent friction in the future.*

Ultimately, the reason output architecture matters is that your impact is determined not just by what you think or say, but by *what you leave behind.* Your systems, your templates, your content, your documentation, these are the footprints of leverage. They outlast your attention. They deliver value long after you've moved on.

Most people are stuck in a world of one-time effort. They push the boulder up the hill every day. High-leverage operators design systems that *roll downhill on their own.*

You don't need to produce more. You need to *design outputs that deliver results* for you.

That's how you stop being the engine and start building one.

Chapter 19, Your Leverage Control Panel

Setting up dashboards to monitor the machine, not micromanage the parts.

Leverage isn't just about building systems; it's about *knowing they're working*. And at scale, that means visibility. You cannot manage what you can't see. You cannot optimize what you don't measure. And you absolutely cannot trust your systems if you're constantly wondering whether they're still running behind the scenes.

That's where the control panel comes in.

The most successful solo operators, creators, and entrepreneurs I know have something in common. They don't just build systems. They make *a way to see the system*. A single source of truth. A high-altitude dashboard that lets them monitor flow, track results, surface risks, and make decisions, without having to poke around in every tool or inbox to do it.

This is your leverage control panel. And without it, your stack is blind.

The control panel is not another to-do list. It's not a productivity app. It's not just a prettier version of your calendar. It's a *strategic overlay*, a dynamic view of the business you've built, how it's performing, and what parts require your attention. It's about stopping the internal workings of your machine and starting to work *on* it.

Let's step into the mindset for a moment.

Imagine you're the pilot of a jet. You're flying high at cruising altitude, systems humming, destination set. You don't need to walk back into the engine room every twenty minutes to make sure the turbines are still spinning. You look at the instrument panel. Fuel levels. Altitude. Pressure. Trajectory. You trust the numbers because the plane is designed to report them.

Your business should work the same way. Your systems, whether for lead gen, content, client delivery, or finance, should surface the metrics that matter. And they should do so automatically, consistently, and in real time.

The problem is that most people don't think this way. They track what's easy, not what's important. They review based on gut feel. They are surprised when systems fail because they never developed a way to detect degradation before it was too late.

A proper control panel fixes this.

You start by identifying your *leverage points*. What are the systems in your business that generate outsized results? Which ones break things when they stall? Where does your attention have the highest return? These are the components your dashboard must surface.

Think in categories, revenue, attention, capacity, and momentum.

Revenue, Are your income-generating systems working? What's your pipeline status? What did you close last week? What invoices are pending? What recurring revenue is projected?

Attention, How is your reach growing? What content performed best? Are your newsletter open rates trending up or down? Where are people engaging most?

Capacity, Are you operating within your limits? How much client work is in flight? Are deadlines being met? Are tasks stacking up in any category?

Momentum, What moved forward this week? What assets were created? What systems were updated? What bottlenecks were cleared?

These aren't just vanity stats. They're indicators of system health. A sharp drop in capacity metrics might mean your delegation engine is breaking down. A spike in momentum might signal that your new workflows are compounding. The key is that you don't need to go digging. The numbers *come to you.*

So how do you build this?

You start by aggregating your sources. Airtable, Notion, ClickUp, Stripe, Google Analytics, social dashboards, Typeform, and CRM tools all hold pieces of the puzzle. Your job is to connect them. Not manually, but through intelligent integration.

You can use no-code tools like Make or Zapier to push data into a central hub. Or use automation-friendly platforms like Coda or Notion to build dashboards that update themselves. The point is to eliminate the need for data-chasing.

The control panel should show current status, trends over time, and exceptions that need attention. Green means go. Yellow means caution. Red means act. This simple triage view allows you to focus *where it matters*, not just where things are noisy.

But the real power of the control panel isn't just in surfacing problems. It's in reinforcing strategic focus. When you see what's working, you double down. When you know what's lagging, you diagnose. And when you see everything moving together, you feel something rare in solo entrepreneurship, *calm control.*

Let's go deeper.

Suppose your podcast production is running through a five-stage workflow, record, edit, schedule, publish, promote. Instead of checking every project board, your dashboard shows how many episodes are at each stage. You see instantly if production is bottlenecked at editing. You act accordingly.

Or maybe you run a content marketing system that posts to five platforms. Instead of logging into each, you track engagement metrics through an integrated dashboard. You notice LinkedIn impressions are climbing while Instagram impressions are falling. You explore why. Adjust strategy.

Now imagine every function of your business operating like this. Each system reports its health. Each workflow surfaces its velocity. Each metric tells a story, not just about performance, but about *design quality.*

Because that's the final layer, the control panel isn't just for management. It's for *system improvement.* When something breaks, it's not a mystery. When something excels, it's not a fluke. Your data becomes a feedback loop for architectural refinement.

That's when leverage compounds.

You start making better decisions because the system tells you the truth. You stop relying on memory or instinct alone. You reduce anxiety because you're not guessing. You reduce overwhelm because you're not checking everything all the time. You move from reactivity to *responsiveness.*

And when the dashboard is dialed in, when it shows you what's happening, what's missing, and what's next, you start to feel something few operators ever experience,

Distance without disconnection.

You're no longer buried in the machine. You're watching it, guiding it, and optimizing it. That's not passive. That's power.

Because the real reason to build a leverage control panel isn't just to track your business.

It's to prove to yourself that you've built something that finally runs on its own.

Chapter 20, Time, Energy, and Attention Routing

Protecting your most valuable non-renewable resources through system guardrails

Leverage isn't only about output. It's also about *preservation.* You can automate workflows, delegate tasks, and scale delivery, but if you lose control of your time, energy, and attention, the entire system begins to corrode. These are your non-renewable assets. And in a world of limitless inputs and infinite pings, protecting them isn't just wise, it's required.

People often treat time as the ultimate constraint, and rightly so. It's fixed. But what they miss is that time without energy is useless. And energy without attention is squandered. You can have eight hours blocked off, but if you're drained or distracted, nothing meaningful will happen. Conversely, a single focused hour, with precise attention and high energy, can move mountains.

This is why every high-leverage operator eventually becomes obsessed with *routing.* Not time management. Not hustle. Routing. The deliberate, strategic allocation of your core resources to where they matter most, when they matter most.

You don't want to control your calendar. You want to design your operating rhythm.

That begins with recognizing one simple truth, your time is already being routed, just not by you. Left unguarded, your calendar becomes a playground for other people's priorities. Your energy gets drained by maintenance tasks. Noisy inputs, false urgency, or digital clutter hijack your attention. Leverage requires *intentional interception* of this default state.

So how do you reclaim it?

First, you define your *peak zones*. Everyone has natural energy rhythms, times of day when you're mentally sharp, creatively fertile, or emotionally present. For some, it's early morning. For others, late at night. The key is not to conform to some productivity gospel, but to identify your power windows and then *guard them like profit centers*.

Once identified, those hours become *sacred real estate*. That's when you write, design, decide, architect, or perform high-value thinking. You do not check Slack. You do not open an email. You do not take status calls. You route your attention like an air traffic controller, deliberate, sequential, and aware of what's at stake.

This may sound rigid. It's not. It's *strategic*. You can still be flexible. But your default posture becomes *protection, not reaction.*

Next comes the layering of systemic guardrails, structures that protect you from drift. Think of these as filters, defaults, and automations that reduce the chance of misallocated energy.

Calendar design is the most obvious. Instead of scheduling ad hoc meetings, you set availability windows. Instead of saying "yes" and finding time later, you design intake processes that qualify requests before they hit your schedule. You use tools like

Calendly or SavvyCal with built-in buffers. You maintain visibility over your upcoming bandwidth, not just for appointments, but for *attention-heavy work.*

You also automate *offloading.* Use delegation engines to route tasks the moment they arise. Create filters that sort messages by sender type or urgency. Set up daily or weekly reviews that batch low-context work together. Your system becomes a moat; only high-leverage, high-context work gets through.

But beyond tools, there's something even more critical, decision posture. You must ask yourself with every request, task, or obligation, Does *this justify my best attention?*

This is not elitism. It's stewardship.

You have a limited number of decisions, a limited supply of focus, and a limited reservoir of drive. Leverage doesn't mean saying "yes" to more. It means building a life where your "yes" is worth exponentially more than it used to be.

Let's talk about *attention design.* We live in an economy that profits from distraction. Every platform, notification, and headline is designed to redirect your attention. So, you build systems to fight back. You turn off notifications by default. You silence inboxes during deep work. You create dashboards that surface only the signals that matter. You log out of platforms that no longer earn their space in your day.

You don't rely on willpower. You *build environments* that make focus easier than distraction.

That environment also includes your information diet. Consuming random advice, reactive news, or shallow content drains attention even when you're not "working." The mind starts to fragment. So, you build a protocol, long-form over fragments, books over feeds, silence over noise. You train your focus like a muscle, not for purity, but for *stamina*.

Let's zoom out.

When you route time, energy, and attention well, your work gains rhythm. Your life gains texture. You know when you're off-duty. You know when you're deep in craft. You know when to rest and when to sprint. This isn't work-life balance. It's a *leverage equilibrium*, a sustainable pattern that produces consistently without burnout.

And yes, rest matters here. High-leverage operators don't just work with intensity. They recover with intention. They treat downtime as strategic fuel. They build in Slack, so the system doesn't tear under pressure. Those slack, those hours, days, or weeks where the calendar is light, aren't indulgence. They're *capacity insurance*.

They're what allow you to surge when it counts.

Let's talk about *tracking* for a moment. Not everything that matters can be measured, but much of it can. You can track where your time goes (RescueTime, Toggl, or even manual time audits). You can reflect weekly on where your energy dipped or surged. You can log where distractions came from. Over time, this becomes pattern recognition. And pattern recognition becomes design intelligence.

You don't guess what's working. You *see it.* You refine your rhythms, cut weak tasks, reroute priorities.

Eventually, you reach a point where your systems are not only protecting your time, but they're also *amplifying* it, where each week feels more aligned. Where your outputs increase, but your stress does not. Where your calendar tells a story of clarity, not chaos.

That's the real win.

Because leverage is not just what you build, it's what you *don't allow to take root,* the clutter, the scattered focus, the invisible drains. When you route your time, energy, and attention with precision, you don't just protect your most vital resources.

You build a machine around them.

And in doing so, you buy yourself the rarest outcome of all, The ability to choose not just *what* to work on, but *how much of yourself* to bring to it, every single day.

PART III, Scaling Without Breaking

Chapter 21, Solopreneur to Systempreneur

Turning your knowledge into scalable value delivery

There comes a point in every solo operator's journey when doing more becomes impossible. The days fill up, the tasks multiply, and every hour you reclaim somehow gets swallowed by something urgent. Your business grows, but so does the weight of maintaining it. What once felt like freedom begins to feel like a cage of your own making.

You may be your boss, but you're also your only employee. And that's not leverage, that's a liability.

The solopreneur path begins with noble intentions—independence, ownership, flexibility. You want to build on your terms. And for a time, it works. You monetize your skills, build a reputation, maybe even hit six figures. But underneath the momentum is a silent constraint, your growth is directly tied to your presence. If you stop working, everything stops.

Eventually, you face a crossroads. Either you scale your effort, which leads to exhaustion, or you evolve your model.

That evolution is what this chapter is about.

Moving from solopreneur to systempreneur is not about building an agency, hiring staff, or becoming a tech CEO. It's about designing a business that no longer depends on your constant attention to survive or grow. It's a shift in mindset from being the product to building the machine that produces it.

The first significant shift begins with how you treat your knowledge. Most solopreneurs hold everything in their heads, decisions, workflows, preferences, and even client logic. It's faster in the moment. But over time, it becomes a bottleneck. You can't delegate what isn't documented. You can't scale what only lives in your brain. So, the systempreneur starts externalizing.

Instead of reinventing the wheel every time, you begin to treat your know-how like infrastructure. You capture how you onboard clients, how you diagnose problems, how you make decisions, and how you evaluate risk. Not to create bureaucracy, but to create clarity. These aren't just notes; they're the foundation of operational intelligence. They become assets, templates, playbooks, workflows, prompts. They become system thinkers like you when you're not there to feel for it.

The second shift is in how you deliver value. In the solopreneur model, you sell time, insight, or craft, and all of it requires your presence. You're in the meeting, on the call, doing the work. It feels noble, even artisanal. But it's a trap. The moment you can't show up, the value flow stops.

Systempreneurs approach this differently. They stop tying value to real-time delivery. That doesn't mean abandoning clients or becoming hands-off. It means designing delivery systems that operate with structure and predictability, ones that can carry 80% of the load without you.

A coaching call evolves into a guided program, complete with a prebuilt curriculum and asynchronous support. A done-for-you service becomes a productized offer with repeatable scope, delivery assets, and predefined timelines. A brainstorming session becomes a diagnostic tool embedded into your website. These are not shortcuts; they're scale mechanisms.

You're still providing value. You're just no longer the bottleneck for delivering it.

The third shift is in how you view your work. Solopreneurs think in terms of output. Projects, tasks, deadlines. They optimize for efficiency, how to get more done in less time. Systempreneurs think in terms of assets. They ask a different question, how do I build something that keeps working without me?

An asset could be a library of onboarding videos. A client dashboard. An AI prompt library tuned to your style—a proposal generator with embedded logic. The common thread is this, assets don't disappear when you stop working. They persist. They compound. They create value independent of your energy.

This shift also changes how you experience time. In solopreneur mode, time is linear. Every hour of revenue costs you an hour of life. In systempreneur mode, time becomes multiplicative. An hour spent designing an automation may save you twenty dollars in the next month. An afternoon building a knowledge base might eliminate fifty future emails. Suddenly, you're not spending time; you're investing it.

And then there's infrastructure. Solopreneurs often build systems around themselves, what works for them, what's fast, what's familiar. But systems based on preference tend to buckle under growth. You forget what lives where. Things fall through the cracks. The system doesn't scale because it wasn't designed to.

Systempreneurs design infrastructure for flow, not memory. They build digital environments where everything has a home, where tools talk to each other, and where the machine moves information seamlessly. Tasks are batched. Emails are triaged. Workflows have states. Inputs are directed to specific locations upon arrival, and outputs occur automatically without manual oversight. Not because you're lazy, but because you're leveraged.

There's a freedom in that kind of structure. Not rigidity, but relief. You wake up knowing the system didn't sleep. You start a day not with dread, but with clarity. You move faster because there's less clutter to navigate. And when something breaks, you fix the system, not just the symptom.

That's what systempreneurs do. They architect solutions, not just respond to problems. They're not driven by urgency; they're led by design.

Perhaps the most significant shift, though, is identity. Solopreneurs often equate their value with effort. They feel virtuous when they're busy, guilty when they're not. But leverage demands that you detach your worth from your workload. That you build something *bigger than your capacity.*

To do that, you have to let go.

Let go of perfectionism. Let go of the idea that no one else, or no system, can do it like you. Let go of the pride that comes from being the only one who knows how it all works.

Because here's the truth, if your business can't operate without you, it's not a business. It's a job you built for yourself. And eventually, it will become the thing that burns you out.

The systempreneur sees it differently. They see their time as precious, their energy as finite, and their knowledge as a resource to be shared, not hoarded. They build not just for themselves, but for sustainability. For transferability. For peace of mind.

And as their system matures, something amazing happens.

They get their life back.

Their evenings. Their weekends. Their clarity. Their ability to focus on what matters. Their ability to think long-term, rather than focusing on short-term survival, is a key aspect of their strategy.

That's the shift.

From reactive to proactive. From busy to intentional. From effort-based to design-based.

From solopreneur, to systempreneur.

Chapter 22, The Friction Audit

Identifying and eliminating bottlenecks before they scale

There is a kind of resistance that doesn't announce itself. It doesn't stop you outright or create an immediate breakdown. Instead, it lingers just beneath the surface, quietly sapping momentum from everything you do. You know it's there, you can feel it, but it hides behind the routine, masked by the familiarity of daily operations. This is friction, the subtle inefficiency that, when ignored, becomes the silent killer of progress.

Unlike a catastrophe, friction doesn't come with warning lights. It doesn't scream for attention. It shows up in the extra seconds it takes to locate a file, the manual process you meant to automate but never did, the email you copy-paste for the fiftieth time because a template was never built. These micro-inefficiencies compound quietly. And over time, they don't just waste hours; they corrode clarity, drain energy, and subtly convince you that business is more complex than it has to be.

This is why the friction audit matters. It's one of the most underrated but high-leverage exercises a systempreneur can do. It's not about finding errors or solving obvious bugs. It's about shining a light on everything that works but does so *poorly.* Everything that "gets the job done," but not without unnecessary friction. In this context, progress doesn't come from adding more, but from *removing drag.*

To understand where friction is hiding, you have to slow down enough to observe. That in itself is a radical act. Most entrepreneurs are moving too fast to notice inefficiencies. They adjust in real time, workarounding instinctively, and normalize every workaround until it becomes the new workflow. And by the time the cost of that friction is clear, they've already paid it tenfold.

The first step is to step back, not with a consultant's eye, but with a designer's awareness. You look at your systems, not for what's broken, but for what's *unnecessarily complicated.* What takes longer than it should? What repeats more than it needs to? What feels heavier than the value it produces? The friction audit starts not with a spreadsheet, but with curiosity.

You pick a workflow, any one that recurs with frequency, and you walk through it like it's the first time. You map the flow from trigger to outcome. You notice how many platforms it touches, how many decisions are required, and how much of the process relies on you to remember, react, or manually intervene. Most importantly, you notice where energy dips. The friction doesn't always live in the clicks. It lives in the feelings of fatigue, the sigh before a task, the silent resistance before engaging with a system that doesn't feel right.

Often, you'll find that friction hides in the seams. It's not the app, but the gap between apps. It's not the task itself, but rather the lack of clear context around it. It's not the conversation, but the three steps it takes to find what you need to contribute meaningfully to it. Friction hides in the decisions you make repeatedly because there's no system in place to make them once and for all. It lives in the follow-ups you chase, the invoices you track manually, and the content you republish by hand because the automation was never set up.

And yet, even when friction is found, many people hesitate to fix it. They rationalize it. "It's not that bad." "It only takes a minute." "I'll fix it when things calm down." But that minute, repeated daily, becomes a week a year. That minor annoyance, tolerated, becomes a quiet form of sabotage. Because it's not just about time, it's about trust in your system. Every piece of friction signals to your brain that things aren't working perfectly. And that signal accumulates.

The systempreneur treats friction like an engineering problem, not a personal one. Instead of blaming themselves for forgetting, they redesign the reminder. Instead of tolerating inefficiency, they build elegance. And elegance, in this context, isn't aesthetic; it's operational smoothness. It's the sensation of moving through your work without any friction.

The audit doesn't end with identification; it demands redesign. And redesign doesn't mean overhauling everything at once. It means choosing one friction point and resolving it with finality. Perhaps it involves replacing a recurring client email with a personalized template that auto-sends with a button. Maybe it involves turning your onboarding checklist into a repeatable SOP linked to a form. Perhaps it's about building a lightweight dashboard to track your content pipeline, rather than switching between notes and reminders.

The moment you solve one point of friction, something subtle happens. You feel lighter. You trust the system more. And you gain back a piece of bandwidth that was previously occupied with unnecessary mental load. Then you solve another. And another. And with each improvement, your system begins to feel not just functional, but *supportive*.

You'll also start to see patterns. You'll notice that certain types of friction, say, context-switching between tools, are recurring across multiple workflows. That insight is gold. It allows you to step up a level and redesign holistically. You might consolidate platforms. You might adopt a single source of truth. You might finally commit to documenting your workflows not for others, but for *your future self*, who won't remember why something was set up the way it was.

At scale, this becomes transformative. Because what begins as removing drag becomes a shift in operating philosophy. You stop tolerating inefficiency as a necessary cost of doing business. You stop assuming that friction is standard. And you start realizing that smooth systems aren't a luxury, they're the foundation of sustainable output.

That's the real gift of the friction audit. It doesn't just make your system faster. It makes it calmer. It gives you back mental energy. It helps you feel less behind. And over time, it reveals a truth most people miss, your business wasn't too complex. Your system was just too noisy.

What emerges from this process is a kind of operational clarity. You start building for your future self. You begin to invest in workflows that don't break under pressure. And you stop patching holes reactively because the structure no longer leaks. You stop optimizing for speed and start optimizing for *smoothness*.

That's the shift. Because real leverage isn't just about adding force. Sometimes, it's about *removing resistance*.

Chapter 23, Designing for Optionality

Systems that adapt with you, not bind you.

Every decision you make in your business either adds freedom or removes it. Every tool, template, or tactic you adopt comes with a hidden cost, rigidity. And while the promise of systems is efficiency, their danger is inflexibility. When we over-optimize for control or speed, we risk designing cages that lock us into patterns we can't escape. The solution is not to abandon systems, but to build them differently, from the ground up, with a bias toward *optionality.*

Optionality is the ability to adapt without starting over. It's the strategic preservation of choice. It means your systems don't just work, they grow with you, bend without breaking, and offer multiple paths forward instead of just one. It's the difference between a brittle process that collapses under new information and a resilient framework that expands as your context evolves.

Most people design systems based on current pain. They ask, "What's broken today, and how do I fix it?" That's useful in the short term, but short-sighted in the long run. Because the business you're solving for today may look very different in six months, and if your system is built too tightly around your present self, it won't serve your future self at all.

The fundamental shift begins when you stop designing systems to *solve problems* and start creating them to *accommodate change.* That means leaving space in the architecture. It means resisting the urge to lock every variable. And it means favoring a structure that is flexible, modular, and dynamic rather than complete, static, and final.

Take content, for example. Many creators build rigid production systems. Monday is idea day, Tuesday is scripting, and Wednesday is publishing. That's fine until a launch changes your priorities, or a collaboration emerges, or you want to follow a wave of inspiration. If the system can't flex, it doesn't help; it hinders. But if your system allows for modular plug-ins, like a content idea vault, templates that can be reused out of order, or automated queues that allow reshuffling without breaking flow, then you remain agile.

Or consider automation. One of the most excellent leverage tools available is the ability to set and forget workflows. But if your automations are built in a linear, tightly coupled way, where each step depends on the previous one being perfect, you've created a dependency chain that can crumble with a single change. Instead, the systempreneur favors conditional logic, loose coupling, and modular design. You don't automate everything unthinkingly; you automate with fail-safes and *decision points* so that the system continues to work even when the context shifts.

Optionality shows up in how you make decisions, too. There's a temptation, especially when you're building solo, to lock yourself into platforms, products, or pricing structures because they're simple. But simplicity without adaptability becomes a trap. For example, committing to a pricing model that doesn't leave room for tiered offerings, licensing, or different client types may streamline your initial pitch. Still, it may also limit your future revenue models.

Optionality would ask, how can I design this pricing in a way that allows for multiple expressions of value? How can I build in the possibility for growth, for productization, for eventual delegation? Not because you'll need those paths today, but because you want the freedom to walk them tomorrow.

This doesn't mean planning for every scenario. That would be its form of paralysis. Instead, it means choosing architectures that invite change. When building your knowledge base, do you use a searchable and linkable format, or do you lock your thinking into static PDFs? When creating your client onboarding, do you allow for different service levels, or do you assume every client will follow the same script?

Optionality thrives on templates that aren't too specific, tags that allow for dynamic filtering, and databases that are designed to be re-sorted and recombined. It's less about adding features and more about leaving space. Not filling in every blank but knowing which blanks to leave open. Not because you're unsure, but because you're *planning for evolution.*

In practice, this often means building *layers* instead of lines. Your core process sits at the center, but around it are optional modules, context-aware triggers, and escape hatches. For example, your product delivery system might default to email, but also be able to publish to a private portal, send SMS updates, or integrate with Slack if the client prefers. Your knowledge capture system might default to written notes, but it can easily be expanded to include voice memos, screenshots, or browser extensions. You're not boxing yourself in. You're creating a multidimensional structure that can flex with your creativity and your clients' needs.

Optionality also means building with reusability in mind. When you write a proposal, do you write it once and toss it away? Or do you structure it so that chunks of it can be reused, repurposed, templatized, or modularized for future contexts? When you deliver a result, is the value locked into one client's experience, or does it create an artifact, a tool, a template, a dataset that can be abstracted and used again?

The systempreneur sees every deliverable not just as an endpoint, but as a seed. Something that, with a bit of care, can generate more outcomes in the future. That's not wasteful. That's *intelligent reuse.* And it only happens when your systems are designed to *notice* what's reusable and allow you to extract it without friction.

There's also a deeper layer to optionality, psychological optionality. When your systems are flexible, you worry less. Your process does not trap you. You don't fear disruption. You don't avoid change because change requires burning everything down. You know your system can stretch, absorb, and evolve. That peace of mind is not trivial. It's one of the most underrated benefits of intelligent system design.

Because the truth is, your business will change. Your market will shift. Your energy will ebb and flow. Your goals will evolve. The only question is whether your systems will support that evolution or resist it. Whether they will hold space for who you're becoming or anchor you to who you used to be.

Optionality isn't chaos. It's not about keeping every door open forever. It's about creating intentional structure *with room to breathe.* You build guardrails, not cages. You design routes, not ruts. And when the time comes to pivot, expand, or slow down, your system doesn't need to be replaced. It needs to be *redirected.*

That's the goal. Not just systems that work now. Systems that *keep working,* even as you grow beyond them.

Chapter 24, Flywheels, Not Funnels

How repeatable motion compounds without effort

There's a point in the lifecycle of every entrepreneur when they realize that effort alone won't get them to the next level. They've built the landing page, written the newsletter, and run the campaign. They've checked every box in the marketing playbook, optimized for conversions, measured open rates, and click-throughs. And yet, something about it feels...fragile.

Funnels, by design, are linear. They require fresh attention to keep moving. You invest effort at the top, including ads, outreach, and content, and wait for the magic to happen. If you stop feeding the machine, the machine stops producing. Funnels are not self-sustaining. They're carefully balanced pipelines that must be rebuilt and refreshed for every offer, every season, every shift in audience.

Flywheels, on the other hand, operate on an entirely different logic. They are systems that get stronger the longer they spin. They build momentum. They do not rely on constant inputs. Instead, they convert energy into sustained motion, repeating, compounding, and self-perpetuating.

The flywheel is not a new metaphor. Jim Collins popularized it in *Good to Great*, but in the world of digital leverage, its implications are far more profound than most entrepreneurs realize. When building for artificial leverage, not just reach or revenue, but repeatable, energy-efficient growth, the flywheel isn't just a nice idea. It's the only idea that scales.

Where funnels are about movement through stages, flywheels are about movement around a center. That center is valuable. Real, repeatable value that feeds the system with each revolution. You're not just guiding people from "awareness" to "conversion"; you're building mechanisms where every touchpoint reinforces the whole. Where one delighted customer invites another. Where one blog post powers ten future automations. Where one documented process reduces friction for the following hundred users.

A flywheel is built when outputs feed future inputs.

Imagine this, You create an instrumental piece of content, a guide, a teardown, a tutorial. Someone finds it through a search or a referral. It helps them solve a real problem. They share it. Others come in. One of them signs up for your list. That person eventually buys your product. After the transaction, they're automatically routed through a thoughtful onboarding sequence. During that journey, they're encouraged to give feedback, which improves your documentation. That updated documentation becomes part of your support engine. Now, future customers need less hand-holding, which frees up your time to create more content. And the cycle continues.

No new ads. No cold emails. Just a system that compounds because every element supports the next.

That's the flywheel.

But building one doesn't happen by accident. It requires a fundamental mindset shift, from campaigns to systems, from sprints to loops, from performance spikes to sustainable motion. The systempreneur stops asking, "What can I do to get more leads this month?" and starts asking, "What can I build once that drives results forever?"

This shift is subtle but powerful. Funnels demand maintenance. Flywheels demand architecture.

And the architecture starts with *capture.* You must build systems that capture your best thinking, your most impactful work, and your highest-performing assets in a way that allows them to circulate. A well-written tweet isn't just a social update; it's the seed of an idea that can become a newsletter, then a chapter, then a framework, then a talk. Every piece of value should have a place to go, into a database, a swipe file, a system where it doesn't vanish the moment you hit "publish."

From there, you need *connectivity.* This is where most creators and entrepreneurs fall short. They build isolated assets, such as a lead magnet here, a blog post there, a product on Gumroad, or a course in Teachable. But nothing talks to anything else. There's no continuity. No flywheel. Just fragmented content islands, each requiring its own marketing and upkeep.

The systempreneur connects the dots. The blog post links to the product, triggering an automation that routes the user to a personalized follow-up. This invitation invites them into the community, which then feeds testimonials and case studies back into the content engine. Each part serves the next. Each output becomes a future input.

Notably, the flywheel mindset also redefines *success*. In a funnel, success is often short-term, Did they buy? Did they click? In a flywheel, success is recursive, Did they stay? Did they return? Did their action strengthen the system?

This is why communities, platforms, and ecosystems outperform one-time products. Not because they make more money upfront, but because they hold attention longer. And attention, when properly structured, becomes momentum. If someone engages with your work, you don't need to win them over again next month. You've already captured their trust, and trust, when respected, compounds faster than any ad spend.

But here's the part most people miss, a flywheel isn't just about the user journey. It's about *your* energy, too.

The solopreneur burns out trying to fill funnels. The systempreneur stays sane by building flywheels. Because the flywheel creates stability. When you're tired, it still spins. When you take a break, it still turns. When the market shifts, your system may slow, but it doesn't stop because its energy is stored not in your calendar, but in your infrastructure.

You create once. You refine over time. And each improvement lasts.

That's not just marketing. That's leverage.

To build a flywheel means you stop relying on heroics. You start leaning on systems. You invest in feedback loops, not campaigns. You prioritize assets over events. You make decisions today that reduce effort tomorrow.

And eventually, the payoff shows up.

You stop panicking over launches. You stop waking up wondering where the next lead will come from. You stop measuring your business by how many hours you worked last week because the system is working, not perfectly, but reliably.

That reliability is what buys you freedom. Freedom to think bigger. To take creative risks. To slow down when needed. To double down when ready. Because you're no longer pushing water uphill. You're spinning the wheel.

And every spin costs less effort.

That's the goal. Not a funnel that fills. But a flywheel that *keeps turning*, even when you step away.

Chapter 25, The Myth of Manual Quality

Why done-by-hand isn't inherently better and often isn't repeatable.

There's a deeply rooted belief among solo operators, creative professionals, and even founders that true quality can only come from manual work. It's the artisanal myth, the idea that what is handmade is more authentic, more precise, and more valuable. This belief runs especially deep in service-driven industries where the personal touch is both a selling point and a symbol of craft. The client expects you, the expert, to be hands-on. The audience believes that only your presence ensures the integrity of the final product. And you, perhaps unconsciously, find pride in being the one who touches every piece of the process.

But over time, this belief stops being noble and starts being destructive. Because what masquerades as care or craft often reveals itself to be control. And what looks like excellence usually masks an inability, or an unwillingness, to design systems that preserve quality without constant manual intervention.

This chapter is not an argument against care or detail. It is not a dismissal of deep work or meaningful craft. It is an argument against the idea that only your manual involvement guarantees high standards. That myth is what keeps talented people stuck. It's what prevents businesses from scaling. And it's what keeps your value chained to your time.

The irony is that many people who insist on doing things manually for the sake of quality are not producing better work.

They're producing inconsistent work. When quality is governed by mood, energy, and availability, you may deliver brilliance one day and merely adequate results the next. Manual work, by its nature, introduces variability. It depends on who you are that day, how focused you feel, and how much sleep you got. And while you may tell yourself that you're optimizing for excellence, you're often just optimizing for involvement.

The deeper problem with manual quality is that it doesn't scale. When you have to touch everything to feel confident in it, your ceiling is permanently capped. You can't grow beyond what your body and mind can personally handle. That means no sabbaticals, no proper delegation, and no exit strategy. Your business becomes a shrine to your effort, admirable, perhaps, but exhausting. And worse, it becomes fragile because anything that relies on one person to function cannot survive the absence of that person.

Artificial leverage demands a different way of thinking. It challenges the assumption that manual means better. It asks you to decouple quality from control and to instead embed quality into systems, tools, and workflows that can produce reliable results, without requiring your direct input every time.

That doesn't mean becoming a robot. It means being a designer. You shift from doing the work to designing how the job gets done. You stop polishing the surface and start engineering the engine. And once that shift happens, something remarkable occurs, quality improves, not because you're more involved, but because the process becomes more consistent.

One of the most powerful questions you can ask yourself is, "If I couldn't touch this ever again, what would need to be true for it to be still great?" That question forces you to translate your standards into structure. It requires you to define excellence in ways that others, or tools, can follow. Perhaps it involves creating a pre-publish checklist to ensure every piece of content meets your editorial standards. Maybe it involves training an AI to mimic your voice and style with sufficient precision, making a first draft feel ninety percent accurate. Perhaps it involves designing your onboarding process to ensure no important detail is overlooked, even when someone other than the intake handler is engaged.

Quality doesn't come from your hands. It comes from clarity. If the expectations are well-defined, if the inputs are structured, and if the feedback loops are tight, then high standards can be met without you being in the room. That's not abandonment. That's leadership. That's what separates operators from owners, tacticians from architects.

Still, there will be resistance. Part of the myth of manual quality is emotional. You believe your involvement signals care. You think it proves commitment. You worry that systems depersonalize the experience. But automation is not the opposite of intimacy. It's what makes intimacy repeatable. When your systems handle the predictable, you have more time to show up personally where it matters.

Consider a service business where every email is written from scratch. That might feel thoughtful, but it's rarely sustainable. Now compare it to a system where every response is templatized but highly personalized based on tags, behavior, or previous interactions. The second version is more scalable, but it also frees up your time to jump on a call when it counts. It makes room for real presence because you're not buried under administrative sludge.

We need to move past the guilt of not doing everything by hand. There is no moral virtue in exhaustion. There is no extra integrity in insisting on inefficiency. The client doesn't care if you typed the entire report manually or used AI to generate the draft, as long as the final product solves their problem with clarity and excellence. The audience doesn't care if your newsletter was hand-coded or assembled from smart blocks, as long as it delivers insight. What matters is the outcome, not the method.

This is not a license for sloppiness. Leveraged quality is not lazy quality. It requires attention up front. It involves testing, iteration, and documentation. It means you spend time building the system until it works as well as you would have, every time. But once it's built, it frees you. Not just from repetition, but from the constant need to be present to ensure things don't fall apart.

And the best part? When your systems become the standard bearers of your quality, you can innovate again. You can step back and think, plan, and imagine. You can improve the whole machine instead of just fueling it with your hours. You're no longer stuck holding up the roof with your bare hands.

That's what leverage makes possible. Not lower standards, but standards that don't degrade with fatigue. Systems that hold the line even when you're tired. Automation that honors your taste and delivers on your behalf. This is how excellence becomes scalable. Not by sacrificing precision, but by codifying it. Not by letting go of quality, but by embedding it into every layer of your work.

When you release the myth that manual equals better, you open the door to a more sustainable version of excellence. One that doesn't punish you for taking a weekend. One that doesn't require you to micromanage every touchpoint. One that finally allows your business to grow without compromising the very standards that made you successful in the first place.

Quality isn't how much you touch something. It's how well you design what touches it next.

Chapter 26, Hiring AI, Not People

When to replace labor with logic, and how to do it ethically

There's a moment every solo operator faces when the sheer weight of work exceeds their available bandwidth. The leads are flowing, the clients are happy, the product is gaining traction, but behind the scenes, the to-do list grows longer than the calendar can accommodate. For most, this moment triggers a familiar next step, hire someone. Bring in help. Offload the parts that no longer fit inside your day. This reflex is ingrained in the traditional model of growth; more work means more people.

But what if the first solution wasn't a person? What if your instinct shifted from expanding headcount to expanding capability?

This is the mindset of the systempreneur. It's not anti-human. It's not about replacing people for the sake of novelty or cost-cutting. It's about asking a different question, what if your next hire didn't need to sleep, didn't require onboarding, and didn't scale linearly with complexity? What if your next teammate was a stack of intelligent systems that could execute, adapt, and even learn, without draining your energy or diluting your vision?

The rise of artificial intelligence and task automation has made this no longer speculative. For the first time, it's not only possible but *practical* to structure your business around digital workers, scripts, agents, bots, and machine learning models that handle everything from scheduling and document creation to lead qualification and customer support. These tools are no longer fringe or futuristic. They're accessible, affordable, and rapidly improving in capability.

The systempreneur doesn't just use AI; they *hire* it. They assign roles, define responsibilities, and measure outcomes. They think not in terms of apps but in terms of functional replacements. Instead of a marketing assistant, they deploy an AI sequence that drafts, edits, and schedules social content based on trending topics and performance data. Instead of a project manager, they implement a dashboard that visualizes bottlenecks, sends reminders, and escalates delays automatically. The mindset is architectural, not operational.

But adopting this approach requires letting go of certain assumptions, chief among them, the belief that people are inherently better at all tasks. This isn't about disrespecting human talent. It's about understanding the difference between human intelligence and artificial efficiency. Some tasks demand judgment, empathy, and intuition. And some tasks require consistency, speed, and pattern recognition. Knowing the difference is where leverage begins.

Start by identifying the repeatable. If you find yourself doing the same task more than once a week, it's a candidate for automation. Not just because it saves time, but because it reduces error, cognitive load, and context switching. A tool like Zapier or Make can bridge platforms without manual effort. An AI assistant can summarize meetings, prioritize action items, and draft follow-up messages. A custom GPT trained on your tone and templates can produce first drafts of outreach or proposals that require only light editing.

Then look at the predictable. Tasks that follow rules, no matter how complex, are ideal for AI. Think about onboarding a new client. If the process involves sending a welcome email, collecting forms, scheduling a kickoff call, and populating a shared folder, each of these steps can be handled by automation. With the proper setup, the only thing you need to do is show up to the call. Everything else unfolds on rails.

This approach isn't just about saving time. It's about *protecting time.* When your systems handle the base layer of activity, your attention can move higher up the value chain. You spend less energy managing chaos and more energy designing leverage. You get to operate from intention, not reaction.

Still, there are risks. Delegating to machines is not without consequences. Poorly designed automation can create messes faster than humans ever could. AI that lacks context can generate flawed or even harmful outputs. That's why the systempreneur doesn't blindly automate. They approach it like any hiring decision, with structure, clarity, and oversight.

You define the role. What outcome do you expect this tool to deliver? How will you measure its effectiveness? What guardrails will prevent unintended actions?

You document the playbook. What data does it need to operate? Where does it pull from? Where does it push to? What happens if it fails? Is there a fallback?

You monitor the results. AI isn't "set and forget." It's "set and supervise." You treat it like a team member in training, capable, but still learning. You observe the outputs, refine the inputs, and improve the system with each iteration.

Perhaps most importantly, you remain ethical. Not every job should be replaced with AI. Not every task benefits from automation. There's a human side to work that cannot be, and should not be, outsourced to silicon. This is where discernment becomes essential. You automate the boring, not the meaningful. You use AI to lift the load, not to erase the soul of your business.

Ethical systempreneurs draw boundaries. They disclose when AI is involved. They avoid deceptive practices, like pretending a bot is a person. They protect user data. They audit for bias. And they never sacrifice trust in the name of convenience.

When done well, hiring AI can be deeply humanizing, not just for the builder, but for the client. Because it gives you the capacity to show up where it counts, when your calendar isn't flooded with tasks a bot could handle, you can focus on strategy, vision, and personal connection. The leverage of machines creates space for the leverage of meaning.

You also begin to see your business differently. You stop thinking of capacity in terms of hours and start thinking in terms of architecture. You ask, what can be built, not just what can be done? Where is the bottleneck, and can it be bypassed with intelligence instead of labor?

Over time, your org chart starts to look different. It's not a hierarchy of people, but a constellation of systems. Some are AI-powered. Some are rule-based. Some are just intelligent workflows. But together, they create a structure that runs with minimal oversight, maximum reliability, and near-zero burnout.

That's what makes this shift powerful. You're not just cutting costs. You're changing the shape of what a business can be. You're building something resilient, efficient, and scalable without sacrificing your sanity. You're rejecting the reflex to hire humans for what machines can do better and preserving human energy for where it makes the most significant impact.

The systempreneur doesn't fear AI. They don't worship it either. They treat it like any good hire, with clarity, with respect, and with boundaries.

Because in the end, leverage isn't about replacing people. It's about using machines to enable people to do what only people can do.

Chapter 27, Decision Infrastructure

How to encode your judgment into scalable processes

Most people think of decisions as moments. Discrete points in time where a person chooses a path, weighs pros and cons, and moves forward. In this view, decisions are events, isolated, personal, and often reactive. But for the systempreneur, decisions are not just moments. They are systems. They are patterns. And most importantly, they are *infrastructure*.

Building decision infrastructure means codifying how you think, not just what you do. It means translating your judgment, preferences, and strategic patterns into systems that others, or machines, can operate. It's the difference between being the only person who knows how to steer the ship and building a self-correcting compass into the helm. When done well, decision infrastructure lets you step away without fear that everything will veer off course. Your logic stays behind, embedded into the system itself.

For most entrepreneurs, this is an unfamiliar concept. Decision-making is treated as a profoundly human function, one that requires nuance, experience, and instinct. And that's true, at first. But what's often missed is that *many* decisions are not one-offs. They're recurring. They're pattern-based. They follow a logic, even if that logic has never been documented. The systempreneur's task is to extract that logic and give it structure.

Begin by examining the decisions you make repeatedly. You'll find them everywhere. How do you price custom work? How do you decide which opportunities to pursue? When you say yes to collaborations. How do you handle refund requests? How do you prioritize features or content ideas? These choices may feel intuitive, but if you've been in business for any length of time, there is likely a pattern beneath the intuition.

The first step is awareness. Begin tracking your decision points—every time you choose A over B, pause. Ask yourself why. What information did you use? What variables mattered? What criteria tipped the scales? If you had to explain your logic to someone else, without being there, what would you say?

What you'll uncover is the raw material of decision infrastructure, principles, thresholds, preferences, red flags, triggers. These are the ingredients of judgment. But they're useless unless you turn them into systems.

That's where decision frameworks come in. A framework is not a script. It's a structured way of thinking that can be applied repeatedly with consistent results. Think of a hiring rubric that scores candidates across five weighted attributes. Or a content evaluation model that prioritizes based on audience need, differentiation, and ease of production. Or a product development filter that only greenlights ideas which are aligned with your core offering, solve a validated problem, and are deliverable within a 30-day window.

The point is not to eliminate human judgment. The fact is to *support* it and to make it transferable. Once a decision framework is externalized, you can delegate the decision itself. You can plug it into an automation. You can build a scoring system. You can even train an AI to apply the same logic. Suddenly, the outcomes are no longer dependent on your availability. They're consistent, explainable, and scalable.

This kind of infrastructure also reduces decision fatigue. One of the most exhausting parts of running a business is not the doing, it's the choosing. Every new scenario demands cognitive energy, Should we launch now or later? Should we take this client? Should we invest in this platform? Without a structure, each question must be answered from scratch. But when you have predefined thresholds, filters, and constraints, the decision becomes faster, lighter, and more objective.

Even more powerful is the ability to stack decisions. Imagine a system where one decision triggers a cascade of others, each guided by logic you designed. A new product idea is scored automatically based on your criteria. If it passes the threshold, a market validation checklist is deployed. If the checklist returns green signals, a launch sequence is scheduled. If engagement meets a specific benchmark, an evergreen version is created. At every stage, the decision has been encoded. You're not making calls from scratch. You're overseeing a machine of your own making.

This kind of infrastructure creates immense leverage, not just in time saved, but in clarity gained. You can see the shape of your thinking. You can refine it. Improve it. Please share it. And most critically, you can *scale it*. This is how a solo operator begins to operate like a team, not by adding more hands, but by embedding more brains into the system.

There's also a defensive benefit to decision infrastructure. It acts as a firewall against emotion-driven mistakes. When stress is high or the stakes are personal, our decisions skew. We justify poor choices, ignore warning signs, and chase novelty. But when your logic is externalized, when the system reflects your best, most deliberate thinking, you're less likely to deviate. You trust the framework, even when your instincts wobble.

Of course, no infrastructure is perfect. And not every decision can, or should, be systematized. There are domains where intuition still reigns. Where ambiguity is too high, or context too fluid. But even in those cases, having *part* of the logic encoded is better than starting from zero. A checklist may not make the final call, but it ensures you don't miss the obvious. A scoring model may not determine your yes, but it can eliminate the easy no.

The goal is not rigidity. The goal is repeatability. You want to create systems that preserve your standards even when your attention is elsewhere. That reflects your values even when you're not in the room. That allows others, or machines, to act with alignment, not guesswork.

And when the infrastructure is in place, something else shifts. You gain confidence. You stop second-guessing. You stop overthinking every move. Because you're not relying on memory or mood. You're relying on a system of thought that was crafted carefully, tested over time, and refined through use.

That's where true freedom begins, not when you escape decisions, but when your choices no longer depend entirely on your presence.

Decision infrastructure is how you scale discernment. It's how you encode judgment into your operations. It's how you turn your brain into a living part of your business, one that doesn't burn out, fade, or get distracted.

It's not the absence of thinking; it's the multiplication of it.

Chapter 28, Leverage That Learns

Training your systems to improve with every use

There's a moment in every builder's journey where they realize that most of their systems, no matter how efficient, eventually hit a ceiling. The workflow that once saved hours now feels rigid. The automation that impressed you last quarter suddenly feels like an awkward workaround. The template, the tool, and the sequence all do what they were built to do. But they don't evolve. They don't adapt. And slowly, what once gave you leverage starts to constrain you instead.

That's the difference between static leverage and *learning leverage.*

Static leverage is helpful. It saves you time, reduces repetition, and delivers consistency. But it remains fixed in time. It reflects the version of your thinking that existed the day you built it. No better, no worse. Just frozen. And if your business changes, your audience evolves, or your own preferences shift, the system needs manual revision or full replacement.

Learning leverage is something else entirely. It's when your tools, workflows, or processes improve over time, *on their own or with minimal guidance.* It's when every user teaches the system something. Every input sharpens the output. Every failure updates the rules. Instead of being built once and forgotten, these systems are designed to observe, absorb, and adjust. They aren't just useful, they're *adaptive.*

This kind of leverage has always existed in high-performing organizations, but until recently, it required expensive enterprise-level infrastructure or massive teams. Today, with the rise of user-trainable AI, modular databases, and feedback-aware automations, learning leverage is available to anyone with the right mindset and a few well-structured systems.

To build leverage that learns, you need two key ingredients, data and a platform where it can accumulate meaningful insights.

That doesn't mean hoarding everything. It means being deliberate. You start by asking, What decisions do I make repeatedly? What choices do I consistently regret? What content, copy, or offers perform best over time? Where am I guessing when I could be aggregating? These are the places where learning leverage thrives because they're feedback-rich, pattern-heavy, and ripe for refinement.

Imagine you run a small course business. Each cohort you launch brings in data, email open rates, enrollment timing, common objections, refund requests, and testimonials. If you treat each of those data points as ephemeral, nothing improves. But if you build a system that logs, tags, and compares them over time, you start to see patterns. You realize that emails sent on Wednesdays convert twice as well. That one module consistently creates confusion, as evidenced by the fact that customers who watch the intro video are 30% less likely to ask for a refund. You're no longer flying blind. The system is learning, and that learning turns into leverage.

This works at the micro level, too. A personal knowledge management system that allows you to tag and resurface notes by context or frequency of access begins to reflect your evolving interests. A custom GPT trained on your tone, voice, and document archive starts producing outputs that feel increasingly like your own writing, not because it was perfect at the start, but because it improves with every revision you feed it. Each prompt, each correction, each iteration becomes a training input. You are not just saving time; you are building intelligence.

That's the power of compounding insight.

Learning leverage doesn't just save effort. It *creates an advantage.* The longer you use it, the brighter it becomes. It starts to anticipate. It begins to adapt. And eventually, it delivers outputs that outperform anything you could have created manually in the same amount of time.

But to get there, you need to do more than collect data; you need to close the loop.

This is where most systems break. Data is captured but never reviewed. Feedback is requested but not integrated. Notes are written but never returned. A system can only learn if its inputs are fed back into its structure. That's what closes the loop. That's what transforms noise into signal. And signal into action.

So, if you want your content system to learn, you don't just track what gets likes; you document what topics get saved, reshared, or cited. You tag your best-performing posts by theme, structure, and tone. You create a taxonomy of insight. And next time you sit down to write, you're not starting with a blank page, you're pulling from a database of what already works, refined by real-world feedback.

If you want your product delivery system to learn, you build a post-purchase loop that captures not just ratings, but friction points. Where did people drop off? What features did they ignore? What language did they use to describe their outcomes? And then you build that insight into your product roadmap, your copy, your support docs.

The more you close the loop, the more your system becomes a living, learning entity.

This is not just about AI, although AI accelerates it. Even simple no-code tools can create learning leverage if appropriately structured. A form that routes inquiries can improve routing logic over time. A decision tree can be updated based on real-world exceptions. A database can show you which offers convert the highest by source or time of year. What matters is not the complexity of the tech, but the intentionality of the feedback architecture.

Of course, there's a balance to strike. Not all feedback is valuable. Not all change is progress. Just because something didn't perform once doesn't mean it's broken. That's why the systempreneur doesn't react impulsively. They observe trends. They compare versions. They analyze with distance. Learning leverage requires patience. But over time, that patience pays off, because each iteration carries forward. Each insight persists. Each lesson becomes embedded.

And unlike a team member who may forget or misremember, your systems don't. Once the logic is integrated, it stays. That's what gives learning leverage its exponential quality. It's not just that you're getting better at using your tools. It's that your tools are getting better *because* you're using them.

This is also where the emotional payoff lives. When your systems learn, you feel less alone. You feel supported. You start to experience your infrastructure not as a passive set of routines, but as an active partner. One that grows with you. One that remembers when you forget. One that evolves as your ambition expands.

You move from merely delegating work to designing *intelligence.* Simply from automating tasks to engineering *insight.* From working harder to thinking sharper.

And the longer the system runs, the better it becomes, not by chance, but by design. That's the kind of leverage that doesn't just scale. It compounds.

Chapter 29, Asynchronous Excellence

Operating across time zones and schedules, even as a team of one

The modern entrepreneur often believes speed is synonymous with simultaneity. The faster you can respond, the more capable you seem. The more you're "always on," the more professional you appear. Responsiveness becomes a kind of performance, a badge of urgency mistaken for competence. However, this way of working, characterized by constant notifications, relentless meetings, and endless pings, ultimately degrades the very thing it claims to support productivity.

Asynchronous excellence is not about working slower. It's about working *smarter*. It's a philosophy that says leverage lives in systems that don't depend on your presence. It's a refusal to build your day around other people's expectations of immediacy. And most importantly, it's how a single individual can operate at the speed and scale of a distributed team, without ever losing clarity, control, or composure.

In an asynchronous system, the work continues when you're not looking. The client gets their welcome email while you're at dinner. The collaborator receives the brief while you sleep. The AI assistant drafts the reply while you're on a walk. Everything is moving, but you're not reacting in real time. You're not caught in the loop of interruption. You are steering the system, not running inside it.

The key to asynchronous leverage is not just delayed communication. It's a *deliberate design*. A Slack message sent after hours is not asynchronous just because it arrives later. Proper asynchronous infrastructure is built on clarity, context, and completeness. It anticipates the unknown. It replaces the need for follow-ups. It's not just a delayed response; it's a complete one that stands on its own.

Imagine you're handing off a task to a designer in a different time zone. In the old model, you'd send a quick message, "Can you update the homepage banner?", and expect a back-and-forth thread of clarifications, What's the new copy? What dimensions? Where should it link? What's the deadline? The task isn't handed off. It's deferred into a limbo of fragmented attention.

But in an asynchronous system, that same task arrives as a fully structured brief, goals, specs, assets, context, and next steps—no meeting needed. No micromanagement. No second-guessing. The work happens while you rest, not just because time zones allow it, but because your system enables it.

The solo creator who embraces asynchronous excellence stops being a bottleneck. They become a conductor. They issue instructions once. They capture context when it's fresh. They rely on systems to surface what matters when it matters. Rules triage email. Notes are converted into tasks. Loom videos replace Zoom meetings. Calendars are structured to reflect focus, not availability.

And what emerges is not chaos, but space.

Space to think, to reflect, to create. Space to move beyond the treadmill of responsiveness and into a rhythm of intentional output. When your systems operate autonomously, your creative bandwidth expands. You are no longer trading your cognitive cycles for urgency tokens. You're building something that doesn't fall apart when you're offline.

This kind of working isn't just for remote teams or global operators. It's especially powerful for solo entrepreneurs who must wear multiple hats without losing sight of the whole. You're the strategist, the marketer, the creator, the customer service agent. If every task requires real-time attention, you end up fragmenting. But if each component of your operation can run with delayed precision, you reclaim sovereignty over your day.

To build asynchronous excellence, you need three core elements, documentation, automation, and expectation design.

Documentation means your thinking lives somewhere durable. It means decisions are recorded, not just remembered. Processes are captured, not reinvented. A new hire, or even future you, should be able to understand what's been done and why, without having to interrupt you for a download. When you record a video instead of holding a meeting, you create an asset. When you write a standard operating procedure instead of explaining something live, you create clarity that compounds.

Automation means your tools do the talking. Follow-ups are scheduled, not forgotten. Reminders are triggered, not requested. Workflows move forward on logic, not availability. A proposal that isn't accepted within a week sends a nudge. A task that remains incomplete triggers a check-in. Your system doesn't need to ask you what's next. It already knows.

Expectation design is perhaps the most underrated pillar. If you want to escape the tyranny of immediacy, you must teach others how to work with you. That starts with clear boundaries. You specify response windows. You define communication channels. You inform clients about the expected update frequency and format. The clearer your norms, the less room there is for misalignment.

This isn't about coldness. It's about consistency. The asynchronous entrepreneur isn't hiding; they're designing. They're choosing presence over performance. They're building a business that respects attention as much as ambition.

Significantly, asynchronous work also enhances inclusivity. Not everyone thrives in real-time environments. Neurodiverse creators, parents with unpredictable schedules, those in different time zones, or with health constraints, all benefit from systems that prioritize clarity over speed. A well-structured asynchronous workflow doesn't just scale productivity. It widens access.

There's a misconception that asynchronous work is slower. In reality, it often moves faster because it reduces friction. When people have everything they need upfront, they act sooner. When a process doesn't require you to approve every step, it moves forward. When rich, structured updates replace meetings, decisions get made without delay.

This only works, though, if the architecture supports it. You need places to store context, not just pass it. Tools like Notion, Airtable, ClickUp, and Loom become your team of one. You link ideas to actions. You surface the right detail at the right time. You stop repeating yourself because the system remembers.

Over time, something remarkable happens, your communication becomes sharper. Your workflows become cleaner. You make fewer decisions in the moment because you've made better ones upstream. The lag between intent and execution shrinks. Your time feels expansive again.

This is not a rejection of collaboration. It's a redesign of it. Synchronous time is still powerful, but it becomes sacred. Reserved for creative collision, not routine transmission. You don't burn it on updates. You use it for breakthroughs. Because everything else already runs.

That's asynchronous excellence, not delay, but design. Not slowness, but structure. A deliberate decoupling of work from time, of action from attention.

You don't respond immediately because you've already responded *intelligently.*

You don't operate in real time because your system operates in *proper time.*

And when the work is still moving while you're making dinner, on a walk, or deep in a book, you realize, this isn't just a better way to work. It's a better way to live.

Chapter 30, Redundancy and Recovery

Building anti-fragility into your infrastructure so you can rest without risk.

Leverage, in its most elegant form, is not about acceleration alone. It's about durability. It's about building a system that doesn't collapse under stress, doesn't fail when you're not looking, and doesn't unravel when something breaks. This is where many highly efficient systems fall short. They optimize for speed, for cost, for output, but not for survival. One loose screw, one missed step, one failed tool, and the whole operation seizes.

Proper leverage demands redundancy. Not because you expect failure, but because you acknowledge reality. Systems break. Files get corrupted. APIs go down. Humans forget. What separates a leveraged business from a fragile one is not how rarely it breaks, but how quickly, and completely, it recovers.

Redundancy, when appropriately designed, is not waste. It is resilience. It is the freedom to pause, rest, or even walk away, knowing the system will not punish your absence with catastrophe. And in the world of artificial leverage, where automation, delegation, and tooling compound your capacity, recovery isn't optional. It is foundational.

The systempreneur builds for failure, not in a pessimistic way, but in a responsible one. They assume the power will go out. They think the email won't send. They take the Zap, which will misfire. Not every time, but eventually. And rather than design systems that require perfection, they design systems that *anticipate imperfection.* That's the heart of redundancy.

At the surface level, this means having backups—data stored in multiple locations. Key documents are mirrored across platforms. Passwords secured through layers, not single points of failure. But redundancy is not just about data; it's about *function.* It's about having multiple approaches for the system to accomplish its purpose.

A newsletter that's scheduled via one tool also exists as a plain-text backup in a folder. A payment funnel that relies on Stripe also has PayPal enabled. A scheduling system that uses Calendly also allows for manual override through a contact form. These aren't inefficiencies. They're layers of protection.

But redundancy alone is not enough. You also need *recovery.* Because even when failure is contained, you must know what to do when it happens. A system that survives a crash but can't reboot is still fragile. Recovery means designing for re-entry. It means documenting what normal looks like so you can restore it. It means knowing what to check, where to look, and how to respond.

This is why systempreneurs are obsessed with visibility. They build dashboards that surface anomalies. They log automation runs, not just outputs. They keep uptime monitors on core systems. Not because they're paranoid, but because they know that what you don't track, you can't fix. Recovery is only possible when you detect the deviation *early enough* to correct it.

Importantly, redundancy and recovery free you from the tyranny of real-time vigilance. The system doesn't need you glued to the controls. Because it was designed not just to work, but to *fail gracefully,* and in that space, you gain something rare for entrepreneurs, peace.

You can leave for a weekend and trust that a server glitch won't erase a month's work. You can spend a day offline knowing that your client onboarding system won't leave new customers in the dark. You can even get sick, distracted, or burned out, and the machine keeps humming.

This is anti-fragility in action. Not just the ability to avoid breaking, but the ability to bend, absorb, and bounce back stronger. A system with built-in redundancy doesn't just survive chaos, it *learns* from it. The failed task becomes a signal. The missed trigger becomes a lesson. And over time, your recovery plan becomes your improvement plan.

There's an emotional dimension to this, too. When you trust your systems, you stop clinging. You stop hovering. You stop believing that your presence is the only thing holding everything together. That's the lie that traps so many founders in cycles of burnout. They build systems that look powerful but are secretly brittle. And because they fear what happens when they're gone, they never leave.

Redundancy is how you reclaim your time. Recovery is how you reclaim your peace. Together, they allow you to scale with calm, not just velocity.

Building this kind of infrastructure requires some uncomfortable questions. Where is my single point of failure? What happens if I disappear for a week? Which processes depend on memory instead of the system? Where do I rely on luck or habit instead of structure? These questions don't reveal weakness. They reveal opportunity.

For instance, if your course delivery relies on you manually granting access, what happens if you're unavailable when the next batch enrolls? Can you move that trigger into an automation? Can you delegate it through a system that doesn't require your password? Or better yet, can you redesign the whole flow so that access is automatic and support is notified only when something goes wrong?

This isn't about paranoia. It's about elevation. You're rising above the noise to build with foresight. You're refusing to trade short-term ease for long-term fragility. And you're doing it not by adding complexity, but by adding *cushion*. The cushion to absorb surprises. The cushion to repair instead of panic.

It's also about *rehearsal*. A recovery plan is only as good as your confidence in it. That means testing. What happens when you simulate a failed email sequence? Do your backups kick in? What happens when a tool disconnects? Does your system alert you, or do you find out when customers complain? Running these drills may seem excessive. But they are what make excellence sustainable.

Because in the end, the strongest systems are not the ones that never break.

They are the ones who *expect* to. And when they do, they do so with grace.

They alert the right person. They retry the task. They escalate the error. They default to safety. They remember how to get back to normal, and then they do.

This is how you scale with sanity. This is how you build a business that doesn't crumble under stress or stall under silence. You design not for perfection, but for resilience. You trade control for confidence. And you realize that true freedom isn't found in flawless operations, it's found in recoverable ones.

Redundancy is not inefficiency. Recovery is not weakness. Together, they are the architecture of sustainable leverage.

PART IV, Sustainable Superperformance

Chapter 31, The Burnout Paradox

How over-leveraged humans fail where systems succeed.

Burnout is often misunderstood. It's not just exhaustion or overwhelm. It's not solved by a weekend off or a better planner. Burnout occurs when internal capacity is consistently outpaced by external demand, leaving no slack in the system, no room for error, and no cushion for recovery. And ironically, the more driven, ambitious, and "high-performing" someone is, the more vulnerable they become. Because at the edge of excellence is a cliff. And many don't know they've reached it until they're already falling.

This is the paradox. The same instincts that build success, intensity, ownership, and responsiveness are the ones that erode it if systems don't balance them. What begins as leverage turns into a load. What feels like momentum becomes obligation. And when people build faster than they systematize, their minds become the bottleneck.

Artificial leverage was never just about scaling output. It was about making performance sustainable. It was about separating ambition from exhaustion, contribution from depletion. But too often, entrepreneurs treat themselves as infrastructure. They become the system, the scheduler, the service provider, the strategist, the support line. Everything flows through them, and because they can hold it all, they do.

Until they can't.

The signs show up subtly at first. You start dropping balls you never used to. Decision fatigue creeps in. A sense of dread attaches itself to things that once felt exciting. You begin optimizing not for impact, but for relief. You're tired, but rest doesn't help. You're working, but the needle isn't moving. The more you try to push through it, the deeper it pulls you in.

And yet, here's the strange part, the machine still works.

The systems still fire. The tools still hum. The automation still delivers. If you've built any infrastructure at all, it doesn't collapse with you. Which means you're left holding a difficult realization, *you didn't have to carry so much alone.* You just didn't let go soon enough.

That's the crux of the burnout paradox, it isn't caused by lack of tools; it's caused by the refusal to trust them. Many high performers will build robust systems only to override them constantly. They'll set up automations, then manually intervene. They'll document processes, then answer every question anyway. They'll delegate, then micromanage. It's not that the leverage isn't there; it's that they don't believe it's strong enough to stand without them.

This is an emotional pattern, not just an operational one. It stems from a deep-rooted belief that presence equals performance. That being involved is synonymous with being valuable. That stepping back means letting down. These beliefs are rarely conscious, but they guide behavior in thousands of tiny ways, replying at midnight, saying yes to every request, staying in meetings that don't require you, rewriting what someone else already handled.

What breaks this cycle isn't more hustle. It's a longer *distance.* It's stepping far enough back to see what the system can do without you. It's giving your infrastructure the chance to prove itself. It's watching the email sequence run, the client get onboarded, the product get delivered, all without your interference. And then I realized the world didn't fall apart. It probably improved.

Burnout often reveals not how much we're doing, but how poorly we've distributed responsibility. In a truly leveraged business, responsibility is shared, with systems, with structures, with rhythms that don't rely on your constant input. The weight is not gone. It's just distributed. That's the only sustainable form of scale.

This shift requires not just delegation, but *decoupling.* You have to decouple identity from output. Worth from busyness. Trust from control. It's uncomfortable at first. You'll feel lazy, even reckless. But then the results speak for themselves. The system works better without your daily meddling. Clients get more transparent communication from templates than from late-night emails. Projects move faster when decisions are structured, not improvised.

What makes artificial leverage powerful is not just that it can multiply your capacity. It can protect your energy. It can insulate your health. It can create the space in which deep work, meaningful rest, and strategic thinking occur. And yet most people only tap into that potential after they've burned out once.

There's a better way.

The preventative approach starts with *load balancing*, not just across tasks, but across time. You stop packing your schedule based on what's possible and start designing it based on what's *repeatable*. You look at your energy patterns, not just your hours, and align your systems accordingly. If your creative output drops after noon, that becomes a rule your workflow respects. If meetings drain you, consider limiting your calendar to two per day. The system doesn't just serve the business; it protects the human inside it.

Next comes *alert systems*. Burnout rarely arrives unannounced. But most people don't have any way to detect it early. A leveraged entrepreneur builds diagnostics into their routine. Metrics like sleep quality, focus consistency, missed deadlines, and emotional resistance to routine tasks aren't just feelings. They're signals. And your system should notice them before they become crises.

Finally, the sustainable path requires *permission to pause*. This is often the most challenging part. Not because the system can't handle it, but because you haven't allowed yourself to believe it will. You take weekends "off" while checking Slack. You book vacations while carrying guilt. You say you've delegated, but you're still monitoring the outcome every hour.

This is not leverage. It's surveillance. And it exhausts you more than the work itself.

When you finally allow the machine to run, you recover something more valuable than rest. You recover *clarity.* You remember what you built this for. You reconnect with the part of yourself that creates, not just completes. And paradoxically, your performance improves, not because you're trying harder, but because you're finally supported by something that doesn't drain you.

Artificial leverage isn't just a path to scale. It's a shield—a safeguard against the burnout that ruins businesses, not from outside failure, but from internal depletion. When used well, it doesn't just make you more productive. It makes you *last.*

And in the end, it's not the fastest who win.

It's the ones who can still think clearly when others have crashed.

It's the ones who kept building even while they were resting.

It's the ones who learned that the ultimate output is *sustainable,* and who designed for it from the start.

Chapter 32, Cognitive Offloading Done Right

Getting tasks and thoughts out of your head and into your machine

There is a moment in every high-performing person's journey when their mind becomes their own worst bottleneck. It's not that they lack ideas, discipline, or ambition. It's that their mental RAM is saturated. Thoughts stack on top of tasks. Ideas compete with obligations. The same items resurface on mental to-do lists day after day, never completed, never forgotten. This isn't forgetfulness. It's cognitive overload. And over time, it corrodes effectiveness, clarity, and well-being.

Cognitive offloading is the act of moving responsibility for remembering, processing, and tracking from your mind into external systems. It is one of the most underutilized forms of leverage because it doesn't look like scale at first glance. There's no revenue number to attach to it. No team member showed up. But what it creates is a silent engine for mental clarity, focus, and creative depth. When done correctly, it doesn't just reduce stress; it unlocks thinking you didn't realize was buried under the noise.

The problem most people face is not that they lack systems. Their systems are scattered, inconsistent, and designed around tasks rather than cognition. They use a calendar for appointments, a notebook for ideas, a whiteboard for planning, a browser full of tabs for inspiration, and a dozen apps for everything else. The mind, in turn, must remember *where* to remember. This defeats the purpose of offloading entirely. What they've created is a fragmented ecosystem that still relies on internal management.

Proper cognitive offloading begins with consolidation. You must choose a single, central hub where ideas land, tasks live, and reminders are surfaced without friction. The tool itself matters less than its architecture. Whether you use Notion, Obsidian, Evernote, Roam, or a physical journal, the principle is the same, it must be reliable, accessible, and trusted. If you do not fully trust the system to catch what matters, you will hold onto everything out of fear, and the load will persist.

The next step is context-aware capture. Many people think of note-taking as a passive exercise, scribbling down ideas or tasks as they arise. But capture is only effective when it includes *why* something was noted, not just *what.* A thought like "email Alex" means nothing in a vacuum. Was it about a project? A follow-up? A conflict? A deadline? Without context, offloading creates confusion instead of clarity. Your future self becomes dependent on your past self's mood and memory. To avoid this, always capture with intent, the purpose, the trigger, the next step. Your system should never force you to decode your thinking later.

With capture in place, the focus shifts to retrieval. This is where most systems quietly fail. The note is saved but never seen again. The idea is filed but never resurfaced. A sound cognitive offloading system is built around *surfacing information at the right moment.* This means integrating reminders, tags, filters, and saved views that bring what matters back into your field of attention without requiring manual digging. It also means routine reviews. Once a week, you sit down and see what you captured. Once a month, you archive or promote ideas based on relevance. This is what turns a note-taking app into a thinking assistant.

The deeper benefit of cognitive offloading is what it makes *possible*, not just what it removes. When your mind is no longer consumed with remembering every deadline, detail, and distraction, it regains space for synthesis. You start to see patterns in your thinking. You begin to cross-pollinate ideas from different domains. You notice which projects keep recurring and which ones quietly die off. You move from firefighting to forecasting. The noise clears. Insight emerges.

This shift doesn't just improve productivity. It changes the nature of your work. Creative breakthroughs often happen not in moments of stress, but in states of mental spaciousness. When you aren't bracing against forgetting something important, your brain relaxes enough to explore new ideas. When your attention isn't constantly pulled by the fear of what you're missing, it can finally go deep. Offloading isn't about doing more; it's about thinking better.

One of the traps people fall into is trying to use cognitive offloading systems as motivational tools. They believe the right app will help them become more disciplined. They load their task managers with color-coded priorities, gamified deadlines, and recurring goals. But when the system becomes too performative, it loses its function. Offloading is not about impressing yourself with complexity. It's about reducing the friction between intent and action. Simpler systems often outperform clever ones because they are used *consistently.*

Another common pitfall is confusing offloading with avoidance. Putting a thought into a system does not absolve you of responsibility for addressing it. You can't delegate anxiety to a note. You can't erase your fear of failure. But you *can* make room to confront those emotions more effectively by removing the mental clutter around them. Sometimes what's overwhelming is not the task itself, but the swarm of unrelated obligations clouding your perception of it. Offloading creates the breathing room necessary to deal with what matters most.

The more ambitious your goals become, the more critical it is to treat your brain like a scarce resource. You only have so many high-quality decisions per day. You only have so much emotional bandwidth. If your mind is constantly taxed by remembering which bills are due, what groceries you need, and which documents you have to sign, then the energy available for strategy, creativity, and connection disappears. The cost of this is not just inefficiency; it's a missed opportunity.

Your cognitive offloading system becomes a form of mental leverage. It is the infrastructure through which your attention is preserved, your focus is protected, and your long-term goals remain visible even when the day-to-day gets chaotic. When built correctly, it acts as a buffer against overwhelm, not just by organizing information, but by *externalizing trust.* You no longer have to hold everything in your head because you trust that the system keeps it for you.

This trust is what makes the system powerful. Without it, you will constantly double-check, second-guess, and over-manage. But with it, you experience something rare, mental stillness amid motion. You feel lighter, not because you're doing less, but because you're thinking less about what needs to be done. The system handles that. Your job is to engage with the right thing at the right time, entirely.

Cognitive offloading, done right, isn't a luxury. It's not an add-on to a busy life. It is the foundation of clear thinking, sustained creativity, and high-output execution. It is how you avoid burnout, not by slowing down, but by *unloading what doesn't belong on your mental desk.* It is how you think sharply, move faster, and rest more deeply.

And it begins the moment you stop trying to hold everything in your head and start designing a system that can have it for you.

Chapter 33, The Myth of Always-On

Why 24/7 output doesn't require 24/7 effort.

The modern entrepreneur has been sold a dangerous illusion, that to build something great, they must always be available. Always reachable. Always working. Productivity is often confused with presence, as if being connected every hour of the day is the only way to remain in control. This myth, the idea that high performance requires constant vigilance, is quietly eroding the very thing it promises to enhance, your ability to do meaningful, sustained work over time.

The truth is that real leverage isn't powered by presence. Systems power it. It's not about how many hours you put in, but about what continues to operate when you don't. Artificial leverage exists to break the link between output and effort. And nowhere is that link more critical to sever than in the idea that being always-on is somehow noble, strategic, or necessary. It's not. It's a liability disguised as dedication.

Being always-on is a recipe for shallow thinking. It forces your attention into reactive mode. Every ping, every email, every update becomes a claim on your cognitive resources. You stop initiating and start responding. You lose the space between stimulus and action, which is where all strategic thinking lives. Even when the work appears to be moving forward, you've lost authorship. You've become a custodian of momentum rather than its architect.

People often cling to the always-on posture because they're afraid of being seen as unavailable or uncommitted. But in doing so, they model the exact behavior they should be eliminating. They create expectations that they find exhausting to maintain. Every real-time reply reinforces the illusion that you are your business. Your energy is the battery, and without it, the system dies. But that belief is not sustainable. It guarantees fragility. And when the crash inevitably comes, it's not just you who suffers; it's your clients, your product, and your long-term vision.

Artificial leverage solves this by designing systems that produce output without requiring your real-time participation. But this isn't just about automation in the technical sense. It's about expectations. It's about training your audience, team, clients, and yourself to understand that your availability isn't the product; your results are.

Availability signals compliance. Boundaries signal competence. The entrepreneur who answers emails at 1 a.m. may seem committed. Still, the one who responds at 10 a.m. with a fully prepared response, supported by a documented system and a straightforward process, is far more effective. Not because they're working harder, but because they're working within a system that respects time, both theirs and others'.

The core shift happens when you stop designing your life around responsiveness and start planning it around rhythm. In an always-on culture, interruptions are constant, context-switching is endless, and the cost is invisible until it becomes unbearable. But in a rhythm-based system, work happens in focused blocks, with intentional handoffs between human and machine, between synchronous and asynchronous, between creation and distribution. The result is not just more output, but higher quality output, created with less emotional and cognitive wear.

Imagine a creator who writes in the morning, automates the publishing workflow by afternoon, and walks away by evening. The content goes live without manual upload. Comments are auto-tagged and triaged by AI. New leads are routed through a CRM and assigned follow-ups without requiring a decision. The system moves even when they rest. And because their schedule isn't consumed by checking, posting, reacting, and refreshing, they re-enter each work session with complete clarity and creative energy.

Contrast that with the creator who feels compelled to check analytics five times a day, to reply to every comment personally, to review every line of copy in real time. They might feel in control, but they're trapped. They've traded leverage for presence, impact for effort, and sustainability for strain. Worse, they've taught everyone around them that this is how things must be done.

Being always-on is not a performance advantage. It's a design failure. It means you haven't built enough trust into your systems. It means you haven't trained your tools or your people to function without you. The solution is not to keep working. It's time to start designing.

That design begins with redefining what responsiveness means. In a leveraged business, responsiveness doesn't mean immediacy. It means *reliability.* Clients don't need you to respond within minutes; they need to know when and how they will get a response, and that the reaction will be complete. The more you codify your response rhythms; the more freedom you gain within them.

Next comes systematized handoffs. Instead of being the single point of approval or execution, you build layers that allow the next step to proceed even when you're offline. This might involve documenting standard decisions, pre-approving templates, or utilizing tools that automatically trigger next steps based on inputs rather than presence. You become less like a gatekeeper and more like an architect. You don't need to push every button; you've already wired the circuit.

This kind of rhythm also protects deep work. It gives you hours of uninterrupted attention, which is the most valuable currency in any creative or strategic pursuit. You don't enter your day asking what needs your response. You enter your day knowing that what matters has been queued, filtered, and presented in a format that enables focus. The trivial and the urgent have been separated. The machine has cleared a path for your mind to do what only it can do.

One of the most important realizations in building artificial leverage is that *you are not your inbox.* You are not your notification feed. You are not the total of your replies. You are the thinker, the creator, the designer of systems that deliver outcomes. And the more you act like a server on standby, the less time you spend doing the work that only you can do.

Letting go of the always-on mindset is not about retreating from responsibility. It's about elevating it. You take responsibility for your time by refusing to let it be fractured. You take responsibility for your clients by building systems that don't depend on your moods. You take responsibility for your vision by preserving your energy for what moves the needle.

This doesn't mean you disappear. It means you show up with intention. You engage in windows of full attention, not as a scattered presence that's always available but rarely effective. You build a cadence, and the cadence builds your results. Everyone around you learns to work with your rhythm, and the respect for your time becomes part of your brand.

In the end, the myth of always-on is not just a cultural norm; it's a personal trap. It flatters your ego while draining your energy. It lets you feel useful while keeping you from being impactful. And the moment you break free from it, you realize something profound, the world didn't need more of your time.

It needed more of your clarity. And that only returns when you stop trying to be everywhere and start building systems that run without you.

Chapter 34, Recovery as a Performance Tool

Creating space to think, reflect, and renew as a systemized habit.

In the world of artificial leverage, it is easy to become obsessed with throughput. The systems hum, the automations execute, the dashboards glow with activity. Everything feels optimized for output. But output alone doesn't guarantee performance. What distinguishes long-term achievers from those who burn out in a flurry of unsustainable intensity isn't just what they do when they're on, it's how they recover when they're off.

Recovery is often framed as the opposite of work. It's what you do when the day ends or the project wraps. But in a high-leverage system, recovery is not the absence of action. It is an integrated, proactive component of performance itself. It's not a reward for output. It's the input that makes output possible at scale and over time. Just as a muscle needs rest between lifts, a systempreneur needs recovery between cycles of deep execution. And just like muscles, without deliberate rest, your mind and systems degrade, not from lack of effort, but from too much of it, unrelieved.

The most dangerous aspect of modern work culture is not the demand for productivity, but rather the glorification of its uninterrupted appearance. The myth that real entrepreneurs never stop, that high-performers are available around the clock, that sleep is optional, and that stress is just another badge of honor. This narrative is not only toxic but also untrue. The highest-performing systems in the world, from elite athletes to billion-dollar businesses, are built on strategic rhythms of stress and recovery. The cycle is not a sign of weakness. It's a design principle.

Recovery, done right, is not reactive. It doesn't wait until you're exhausted to intervene. It is pre-programmed, embedded into the system, and protected with the same level of care as a product launch or a sales funnel. In artificial leverage, this means building recovery into your workflows, your weeks, and your infrastructure. It means architecting a business that doesn't panic when you step away. And it means trusting that rest is not time lost, it's capacity gained.

The first layer of recovery is physiological. You cannot separate your brain from your body. No system, however intelligent, can run on a chronically depleted human. Sleep, nutrition, and movement are not personal concerns to be addressed outside the work system. They are part of the system. If your operating model requires you to neglect these foundations, it's not a high-performance model. It's a high-cost gamble.

The second layer is cognitive. This is about how often and how deeply you give your mind space to disconnect from the logic loops of production. In an always-on, input-saturated environment, your mental processing doesn't slow down when you stop working; it lingers, loops, and replays. Recovery means actively changing cognitive gears. It's not enough to stop writing, coding, or presenting. You need rituals and environments that signal to the brain, the loop is complete, and no background processing is required. Walks without podcasts. Journals without agendas. Hobbies without monetization goals. These are not indulgences. They are maintenance protocols for sustained clarity.

The third layer is emotional. Every decision, even when automated, carries residue. Every client interaction, every team update, every missed metric leaves a trace in the emotional ledger. Without space to metabolize these experiences, the stress compounds. Not loudly, but steadily. Recovery here means reflection. It means systems that help you process, not just track—debriefing after launches and writing about what worked and what didn't—naming the tensions instead of ignoring them. When these habits are part of the system, they catch emotional wear before it becomes psychological collapse.

What makes recovery powerful in leveraged systems is that it scales with you. You no longer need to rely on remembering when to rest. The system can signal it. Your calendar can be structured with recovery blocks, not as optional "buffer time" but as immovable, protected rituals. Your dashboards can include not just KPIs, but RPMs, objective performance metrics, like focus quality, decision clarity, and creative readiness. You begin to see recovery not as absence, but as presence in a different mode. You are doing something vital, even when it looks like you're doing nothing.

There is also a strategic layer to recovery that is often overlooked. When you step back, your perspective widens. You stop optimizing for the next hour and begin designing for the following year. Many of the most critical insights in a business do not come in the middle of sprints. They come in the stillness that follows. The pivot that saves a launch. The redesign cuts the workload in half. The insight that transforms a service into a scalable product emerges in these moments when you give your mind room to reorganize itself beyond the noise of the day-to-day.

And then there is the final layer, reputational. When you build a business that runs with integrity, even when you are not visibly grinding, you model a kind of leadership that is magnetic. Clients trust systems that don't require heroics. Teams respect boundaries that reflect internal coherence. You are not just delivering results; you are providing proof that sustainability and excellence are not at odds.

To embed recovery into your leveraged business is to treat yourself as an essential asset, not just a resource to be spent, but an element to be maintained, protected, and enhanced. You wouldn't run a machine at full speed without lubrication. You wouldn't run code without error checks. So why build an empire on the back of a burnt-out operator?

This shift begins with designing for absence. What does your system do when you're not there? What continues, and what stalls? Where do you insert your energy because it's needed, and where do you insert it out of habit or insecurity? These questions are not about removing yourself entirely. They're about understanding where your presence is a multiplier, and where it's a patch for bad architecture.

Once you identify the points where recovery is blocked, you build alternatives. An automation that sends client updates during your off days. A library of answers that keeps support consistent even when you're offline. A rule that no meetings are scheduled during your focus weeks. A metric that measures depth, not just velocity. Each layer frees you from the cycle of burnout, not by slowing you down, but by providing you with better support.

Recovery is not an afterthought. It is not what you do once the work is done. It is part of the work. It is the reset switch that keeps the engine clean, the perspective sharp, and the operator healthy. In a system designed for artificial leverage, recovery is a feedback loop, not a detour.

The most powerful businesses are not those that run fastest, but those that can run longest. And that endurance doesn't come from grit alone. It comes from recovery built into the core.

You are not a machine. But if you build your systems right, they will protect you like one. And in that protected space, you will find what most entrepreneurs rarely do, the clarity, energy, and longevity to build something that lasts.

Chapter 35, Boundaries by Design

Letting your systems say "no" for you.

In the early stages of a business, boundaries often feel like a luxury. When you're hungry for momentum, exposure, validation, and revenue, it's tempting to say yes to everything. Every inquiry is a possibility. Every meeting is a potential breakthrough. Every request feels like it could lead to something bigger. And for a while, it works. Responsiveness feels like progress. Availability feels like momentum. But eventually, it becomes clear that this constant openness is not sustainable. What begins as a hustle soon becomes erosion not just of your time, but of your clarity, your standards, and ultimately, your vision.

This is the inflection point where boundaries cease to be optional. In a leveraged system, boundaries are not walls that keep people out. They are filters that keep your energy aligned with your intent. They are the protocols by which you protect your best thinking. And when embedded correctly, they are not enforced through confrontation or apology; they are implemented through design.

The power of artificial leverage is that it enables boundaries to be systemic rather than emotional. Instead of relying on willpower to say no, or on awkward conversations to decline misaligned opportunities, your system becomes the spokesperson for your standards. Your workflows reflect your values. Your automation signals your limits. Your communication frameworks establish expectations long before you ever have to explain yourself. This is the quiet genius of boundaries by design, they remove the friction from protecting what matters.

It begins with clarity. You cannot design boundaries around vague preferences. You must decide what is non-negotiable, including your deep work windows, recovery cycles, decision thresholds, and client fit criteria. These are not arbitrary. They emerge from lived experience. You learn where your energy spikes and where it drains. You see what types of interactions move the business forward and which ones dilute your focus. Once these patterns are clear, the job becomes not to hold them in your mind, but to embed them into the fabric of your operations.

Take communication, for example. If you know that checking email before noon derails your creative flow, you don't just try to resist the urge. You set an auto-responder that confirms receipt, outlines response windows, and redirects urgent matters. You train your calendar to avoid stacking meetings back-to-back. You use intake forms that ask clarifying questions upfront, so you don't get pulled into exploratory calls that lead nowhere. Every one of these systems acts as a boundary, and none of them requires you to muster the energy to say no in real time.

This extends to clients and collaborators. One of the most damaging myths in entrepreneurship is that being client-centric means being client-controlled. It doesn't. Respectful service is not the same as unlimited access. Boundaries by design mean you articulate what's included in your offer, how support is delivered, when feedback loops occur, and what turnaround times are realistic. You don't hope people will understand. You design for it.

You give them the tools to succeed within the framework you've chosen to operate in. And in doing so, you attract the kinds of people who value your time as much as you do.

Systems are the enforcement mechanism for this clarity. They are how you build friction around the wrong things and flow around the right ones. A system that books calls only on specific days. A project management tool that filters requests through stages. A proposal template that includes boundaries around revisions, response times, and decision authority. These aren't bureaucratic. They are liberating. They free you from ambiguity, from over-explaining, and from overextending yourself out of guilt or politeness.

The deeper reason boundaries are rigid is emotional. Saying no feels like rejection. It feels like failure to deliver, even when the ask is unreasonable. But when boundaries are encoded into systems, the emotional sting is removed. It's not personal, it's policy. It's not a dismissal, it's a structure. And the more consistently the structure is upheld, the more confident and centered you become. You stop questioning every decision. You stop renegotiating every standard. You begin to trust that the rules you've created are not constraints; they are commitments to your highest leverage.

There's also a strategic advantage to boundaries by design. They create data. Every time someone hits a boundary, your system records it. You begin to see patterns in what people ask for, where confusion arises, and where exceptions get requested. This becomes a feedback loop, not just for improving your operations, but for refining your messaging, your onboarding, your product-market fit. Boundaries are not barriers to opportunity. They are indicators of alignment.

And in a systematized business, they become your brand. People come to respect your time because it's apparent that *you* appreciate it. They don't expect 24/7 access because your communication makes clear that quality is tied to rhythm, not immediacy. They don't assume scope creep is tolerated because your contracts and workflows have built-in safeguards. You become known not for being easy to access, but for being excellent when you engage. And that distinction is the hallmark of sustainable authority.

Another overlooked benefit of boundaries is that they allow you to create more than you ever could if you were constantly available. The world rewards creators who produce from clarity. If every request interrupts your flow, if every day is a negotiation between your schedule and someone else's urgency, you will never build anything truly original. You may stay busy. You may remain visible. But you won't stay ahead. Systems give you back your edges. Boundaries let you keep them sharp.

This is particularly vital in a digital world where presence is often confused with participation. You don't need to respond in real time to be reliable. You don't need to be active in every channel to be respected. What matters is that the systems speak on your behalf, and that they do so with integrity. A templated proposal that sets expectations. An AI assistant that handles first-line support. A content schedule that delivers insight even when you're offline. These are forms of communication that respect your time and the audience's.

None of this means you become inflexible. Boundaries by design *increase* your flexibility. Because when the default system protects your time, you can make conscious choices about when to override it. You can say yes to something outside the norm without it being a pattern. You can make exceptions without compromising the whole. The key is that these exceptions feel like a gift, not a gap. They are deliberate deviations, not signs of inconsistency.

In a leveraged life, every yes carries a cost. The difference between burnout and sustainable momentum is not how hard you work; it's how you decide what *not* to do. Boundaries by design ensure that those decisions aren't made in the moment, under pressure, with frayed nerves and an overfull calendar. They are made in advance, from a place of clarity, and executed by the systems you trust.

And once you trust those systems, you'll notice something remarkable. The people around you start to rise to meet your standards. Clients get clearer. Partners become more self-sufficient. Your audience respects your cadence. And most importantly, you reclaim the energy to lead, not from defense, but from design.

Chapter 36, Emotional Leverage

Outsourcing not just effort, but stress, uncertainty, and repetition

Most conversations around leverage focus on time, money, and technology. Rarely do they confront the emotional toll of sustained performance. Yet behind every broken system, abandoned project, or spiraling workload is not just inefficiency, it's emotional weight that was never accounted for. The stress of decisions left unmade. The anxiety of uncertainty repeated daily. The friction of having to explain, persuade, and validate over and over again. These are not just nuisances. They are leveraging leaks. They erode clarity, burn energy, and eventually cause the entire machine to seize.

Emotional leverage is the discipline of designing your work and systems to absorb emotional load without requiring your constant intervention. It is the act of intentionally offloading stress, uncertainty, and repetition, not by suppressing them, but by building structures that handle them on your behalf. If physical leverage allows you to lift more with less, emotional leverage will enable you to *endure* more with less cost to your peace, confidence, and focus.

We tend to associate emotional exhaustion with intensity, but often it stems from ambiguity. A hundred micro-decisions, unclear priorities, scattered obligations, all of them quietly drain your ability to stay decisive. You can automate a task, delegate a responsibility, or even eliminate a meeting. However, if your systems still make you anxious about whether it's done correctly, you haven't truly offloaded the work. You've only shifted its location.

Emotional leverage starts with clarity. Not clarity in the abstract sense, but clarity made tangible. Decision trees, standard operating procedures, and pre-approved templates are not just time-savers. They are anxiety reducers. They transform situations that once required mental negotiation into structured outcomes. Instead of wondering how to respond to a client request, the answer is embedded in a flow. Instead of worrying whether a team member understood the expectation, the process enforces alignment. You are no longer the bottleneck for certainty; your system is.

This is not about removing emotion from your business. It's about directing it with precision. High-stakes situations still exist. Creative friction still arises. But the difference is that you've reserved your emotional bandwidth for the things that truly require it. You're not using your strategic mind to triage a missed calendar invite or second-guess a formatting choice. You've systematized the low-stakes decisions, so your full presence is available for the moments that matter.

Another area where emotional leverage becomes transformative is in repetition. Saying the same things over and over, onboarding new clients, explaining your process, reminding people of your availability, and defending your value —these micro-repetitions wear on your psyche more than you realize. They breed resentment, fatigue, and eventually apathy. When you codify these messages, through automated sequences, video explainers, onboarding portals, or templated scripts, you're not just saving time. You're preserving patience. You're conserving the emotional energy required to engage meaningfully.

There's also the matter of interpersonal dynamics. Many entrepreneurs spend as much emotional energy managing people as they do building products. But often, this burden stems not from the people themselves, but from a lack of systematized expectations—emotional labor spikes when roles are unclear, when priorities shift midstream, or when feedback is inconsistent. By embedding clarity into your systems, scorecards, cadences, and transparent checklists, you make relationships smoother, not because you're less human, but because you're more structured.

In high-output environments, emotional leverage also comes from temporal design. Not all emotions need to be addressed immediately. Some need to be contained until they can be processed in context. When you build systems that absorb feedback, track anomalies, and surface reflection at the proper intervals, through weekly reviews, monthly retrospectives, and quarterly strategy sessions, you stop reacting in real time and start reflecting in rhythm. This containment doesn't suppress your emotions. It protects your judgment.

What many forget is that emotions are not an externality to business. They are the context in which every decision occurs. If your systems are constantly placing you into emotional whiplash, from elation to stress to confusion to fatigue, you will eventually lose strategic altitude. You'll be reacting, not directing. Emotional leverage ensures that the external noise of your operations does not dictate your internal state.

Consider how trust plays into this. A system that consistently delivers what it promises builds not just efficiency, but calm. You stop needing to double-check. You stop rehearsing worst-case scenarios. You begin to move with a kind of settled confidence that compounds over time. Emotional leverage is this confidence, codified. It is the result of knowing your systems not only work, but that they absorb chaos before it reaches you.

This is why emotional leverage is not a soft skill. It is a hard edge. The entrepreneur who operates with emotional volatility, no matter how talented, will eventually exhaust themselves or repel others. But the one who designs systems that catch emotional friction before it becomes drama, who turns uncertainty into process and stress into structure, becomes formidable. They can operate in complexity without becoming chaotic.

It's also where the real longevity of artificial leverage emerges. Anyone can build a sprint-based system that drives results for 90 days. But to maintain high performance over the years, you must ensure emotional sustainability. This means routines that allow decompression. Workflows that reduce ambiguity. Agreements that prevent rework. And most importantly, a cadence of reflection that turns emotion into intelligence, not interference.

The irony is that many resist emotional leverage because they believe it's a sign of weakness to design for ease. But in reality, the strongest systems are the ones that reduce unnecessary suffering, not by avoiding work, but by making the emotional experience of work more stable, predictable, and affirming. Just as you wouldn't lift a heavy weight without a lever, you shouldn't carry the emotional burden of your business without support.

Building emotional leverage is not about removing feeling from your work. It's about designing your business in a way that protects your emotional fuel. So that when the real challenges arrive, the ones that test your values, your resilience, your vision, you can meet them fully. You are not drained by avoidable tension. You are not consumed by repeated confusion. You are not acting out of fatigue. You are choosing from a place of composure.

And in that composure lies power. The power to lead with steadiness. To make decisions that outlast the mood of the moment. To attract collaborators who respect clarity over chaos. To create work that is infused not with panic, but with presence.

Because in the end, artificial leverage isn't just about doing more with less. It's about feeling less burdened while building more. And the most advanced system you'll ever create is the one that protects your ability to show up, not frantic, not reactive, but ready.

Chapter 37, The Liberation Protocol

Using tools to escape the trap of high-output dependency

It's an irony that haunts high performers, the better you get at doing, the harder it becomes to stop. What begins as discipline becomes entrapment. You are no longer building systems to support your freedom; you are maintaining systems to support your identity. And at some point, you realize your success does not liberate you. You're imprisoned by it.

This is the trap of high-output dependency. When your systems are optimized for output but not for liberation, you become an operator of your constraints. You build more, produce faster, scale wider, but you do so in a cage of your own making. It's a beautiful cage, sophisticated and sleek, but a cage, nonetheless. Every lever you've pulled, every process you've refined, every tool you've wired now serves to reinforce your role as the indispensable driver. And the more vital you are, the more you remain at the center.

The Liberation Protocol is the deliberate unwinding of that center-of-gravity thinking. It is a shift in posture from "how do I get more done?" to "how do I build so I can eventually disappear?" It's not about abandonment. It's about detachment, from ego, from over-identification, from the performance treadmill. It is the art of designing your business and your systems in such a way that your absence enhances the system rather than threatens it.

To begin implementing the Liberation Protocol, you must first confront the part of you that conflates presence with control.

Many entrepreneurs hold a subconscious belief that being involved equals being effective. They are in every meeting, approve every deliverable, and mediate every issue, not because the system requires it, but because their self-concept does. Letting go feels like a loss of power. But in a leveraged system, letting go is where real power is born.

Liberation begins with documentation, not just delegation. You're not simply handing off tasks; you're transferring ownership of logic, thresholds, and intent. Every time you answer a question more than once, write it down. Every time you make a decision based on a principle, articulate the principle. You are not just offloading labor. You are externalizing judgment. This is how intelligence becomes infrastructure. The system stops asking you and starts thinking like you.

The next layer is abstraction. This is where you pull yourself out of the specifics and into the architecture. Instead of optimizing the sales email, you design the lifecycle. Instead of tweaking each client workflow, you create the operating system they all use. Instead of managing the timeline, you build the rules that govern it. You move from working *on* the machine to sculpting the machine itself. The goal is not to step away from the business emotionally; it's to step back from it structurally.

This shift is often blocked not by skill but by story. The story that your hustle is noble. Your input is irreplaceable. The reason things work is that *you* are the one behind the curtain. But this mythology must be dismantled if true liberation is the aim. Because the more the system needs *you*, the more fragile it is. And the more fragile it is, the more it owns you.

Liberated systems are designed to flex, not flinch. They are tested for your absence, not just tolerated in it. You begin asking different questions, What still functions when I don't log in for a week? What continues to deliver value when I take my hands off the wheel? What quality controls persist without manual input? These are not hypotheticals. They are design criteria.

One of the most potent tools of liberation is asynchronous thinking. Not just working on your own time but building systems that *progress* without needing you to signal the next step. This means designing flows that trigger based on logic, not presence. Conditional automations. Escalation rules. Recurring evaluations. The system breathes without you. It doesn't pause when you unplug. It self-regulates.

Another vital concept is asset elevation. Every piece of work you do should feed a future version of you. If you write something, make it reusable. If you solve something, make it teachable. If you design something, make it scalable. You are not building assets for this week. You are building compounding infrastructure. Liberation is not built in one moment. It is the result of a thousand micro-decisions to invest effort in ways that reduce future attempts.

The emotional layer of the Liberation Protocol is perhaps the most counterintuitive. It is the discipline of mattering less. You start celebrating the fact that you weren't needed. That the system solved it. The client was delighted without a call. That your ideas shipped without your signature. At first, this feels like detachment. It can even feel like irrelevance. But over time, you begin to recognize it for what it is, sovereignty.

Sovereignty is not freedom from responsibility. It is freedom from *dependence.* You are responsible for the vision, the design, and the cadence. But you are no longer accountable for propping it up with your constant energy. You are not the engine. You are the architect. And when the engine runs without you, your leverage becomes limitless.

There is a cultural resistance to this posture. We reward the always-on founder. We mythologize the hands-on operator. But this worship of presence has a cost. It creates a generation of burned-out builders who can't leave what they've built. Who can't go a day without logging in? Those who take their laptops on vacation not because they have to, but because the business has never learned how to breathe without them.

The Liberation Protocol is the antidote. It says, You do not have to vanish, but you do need to plan for it. You do not have to abandon the work, but you must not confuse yourself with the work. The system is not you. It is a reflection of your clarity, not your calendar. And the more that reflection becomes autonomous, the more your calendar becomes your own again.

Ironically, the more you implement the Liberation Protocol, the more value you create. Because instead of injecting effort into every transaction, you inject intelligence into every process. Your systems become smarter, not just faster. Your decisions become encoded, not repeated. Your vision becomes expansive, not reactive.

And you, the systempreneur, regain what is so often lost in the pursuit of scale, your optionality. You can go deeper into strategy. You can explore new verticals. You can disconnect for weeks without fear. Not because you escaped work, but because you embedded wisdom into your infrastructure.

Liberation is not a finish line. It is a muscle. You flex it every time you replace obligation with design. Every time you write the playbook, instead of playing the role. Every time you build a system that teaches instead of one that depends, you're making a significant difference. In doing so, you transform not just your business, but your relationship to it.

Because the fundamental goal of artificial leverage was never to scale, it was to give you your life back while you build. And with the Liberation Protocol in place, that vision finally becomes real.

Chapter 38, The Digital Retreat Principle

How to step away while everything keeps running

In a world obsessed with being always-on, the idea of a digital retreat sounds either indulgent or irresponsible. Entrepreneurs pride themselves on responsiveness. Creatives build their identity around real-time publishing. Executives measure value in availability. But what if the real test of leverage isn't how well your system performs while you're present, but how gracefully it operates when you're not?

The Digital Retreat Principle is not about going offline for the sake of rebellion. It's not a vacation in disguise, or a moment of detox before diving back into dysfunction. It is a design philosophy, build your business so that stepping away becomes a form of strategic power, not a liability to be managed. The digital retreat is not an escape. It is a demonstration. When you withdraw your presence and the system keeps humming, you reveal the actual depth of your leverage.

Most people believe they can't step away because the machine will break without them. But more often, the machine breaks *because*they never step away. Absence reveals dependency. It shows you where the logic was in your head instead of in your workflows. It reveals which clients were relying on your availability rather than your systems. It uncovers the redundancies you never built because you never imagined leaving. And this is precisely what makes the retreat so valuable. It isn't a luxury, it's an audit.

Designing for a digital retreat begins long before the retreat itself. You don't just disappear and hope for the best. You build a simulation. You remove yourself from processes one layer at a time. You assign responsibility to automations, to documented playbooks, to asynchronous communication tools. You examine every touchpoint and ask, Does this require my presence, or just my preparation?

Preparation is the first line of liberation. If your business still relies on synchronous input — your approval, your green light, your clarification — it is not yet retreat-ready. You must build default states into your systems. Default decisions. Default expectations. Default permissions. This doesn't mean you never intervene. It means that if you didn't, the machine wouldn't stall. It would adapt, resolve, and continue forward based on principles, not panic.

One of the key enablers of the Digital Retreat Principle is trust, not just in people, but in process. Trust that the email sequence will onboard the client without needing a welcome call. Trust that the documented SOP will guide the assistant without needing check-ins. Trust that your calendar is guarded by rules, not by constant oversight. This trust is not unquestioning optimism. It is earned through testing, reflection, and continuous refinement. The only way to build it is to try stepping back, see where things wobble, and fix the fragility until the wobble disappears.

The emotional tension of stepping away is not trivial. Many entrepreneurs feel guilty not working, even when there's nothing left to fix. But guilt is often a symptom of identity conflict. If your value has always been expressed through effort, then detachment feels like neglect. This is where the mindset must evolve. The digital retreat is not an abdication of responsibility. It is the exercise of design authority. You are not avoiding work; you are confirming the work has been correctly delegated, automated, or made irrelevant.

There is a profound difference between *disconnection* and *distancing.* Disconnection is reactive; it happens when you crash. Distancing is strategic; it happens when you plan. The digital retreat is about creating a scheduled, healthy distance from the system you've built, so that it can become anti-fragile in your absence. And anti-fragility is the ultimate leverage. It doesn't just survive volatility. It gets better because of it.

When you return from a digital retreat, you don't re-enter in the same way. You look at the system from a new altitude. You spot the areas that improved because you weren't there micromanaging. You notice where communication broke down, where questions accumulated, and where decisions were delayed. This becomes data. You don't get angry at the breakdowns. You get curious. Every failure is an invitation to make the system more robust. Every success is a signal that your design is working.

A well-executed digital retreat has ripple effects. Your team, if you have one, becomes more empowered. They stop deferring to you. They build initiative into their thinking. Clients stop expecting immediate responses and begin to appreciate thoughtful ones. Your audience learns that silence does not mean absence; it means maturity. Your business evolves from a personality-driven brand to a principle-driven machine.

Even if you operate solo, the digital retreat transforms how you think about capacity. You begin to measure success not in output volume but in residual output. What continues without you? What content keeps delivering? What product keeps serving? What funnel keeps converting? The more these mechanisms operate in your absence, the more you can focus on the long view, innovation, redesign, and exploration. These are the pursuits that require vision, not vigilance.

There is a common fear among entrepreneurs that they will disappear and be forgotten. But the truth is, when your systems are designed with intelligence, your presence is always felt, even when you're not available. Your ideas circulate in your content library. Your reputation is embedded in your customer experience. Your values are mirrored in your workflows. Presence is not proximity. It's the precision of design.

Practically speaking, the digital retreat doesn't have to be dramatic. It could be a weekend with your phone off, a week without client calls, or a month where everything runs on schedule without your input. The size of the retreat is less critical than its intention. What matters is that the retreat is not an afterthought. It is built into your quarterly cadence. It is protected on your calendar. It is normalized inside your culture, whether that culture is just you or an entire remote team.

There is an additional benefit to digital retreats that few anticipate, creative recovery. When the noise stops, your thinking deepens. When you're not reacting, you start imagining. It's in the quiet that the next chapter of your strategy often appears. Not forced. Not squeezed between meetings. But rising naturally in the space you've reclaimed. The retreat becomes not just a performance test, but a thinking ritual.

And when you return, your decisions are cleaner. Your energy is sharper. You stop overengineering. You simplify. You trust. This is the cycle that sustains not just performance, but the person behind it. Without it, even the most sophisticated system becomes brittle. With it, even the most complex infrastructure becomes serene.

The Digital Retreat Principle reminds us that proper leverage is not about being plugged in. It's about being intentional. You are not building systems to hold you captive. You are building them to set you free. Free to think. Free to rest. Free to grow. And most importantly, free to lead, not from the center of every function, but from the clarity of the edge.

Chapter 39, Teaching the Machine

Training systems once, so you don't have to teach people repeatedly.

For most of history, knowledge transfer meant repetition. You taught a person, they internalized it, and if they left, the knowledge went with them. Every new hire meant starting over. Every change required a meeting. Every nuance lived inside someone's brain or in the subtext of how things were done. Businesses didn't just run on systems; they ran on memory. And memory, while powerful, is volatile.

Artificial leverage changes this equation. When you begin teaching the machine instead of the person, you create systems that retain, refine, and replicate knowledge without erosion. Teaching the machine is not about replacing people. It's about replacing repetition. It's about encoding your best thinking, clearest decisions, and highest standards into structures that don't forget, don't fatigue, and don't interpret things differently on a bad day.

The fundamental shift begins when you start treating your systems as students, not just servants. Instead of building tools that execute, you start building tools that *learn*. Not artificial general intelligence, but practical, embedded intelligence. A well-crafted prompt. A conditional rule. A dynamic automation. A structured intake form that asks the same questions you would ask. These are small acts of knowledge transfer that collectively reduce your need to be present in the loop.

Teaching the machine starts with specificity. You cannot outsource what you haven't articulated. Vagueness breeds inefficiency, whether in people or processes. When you document how something should be done, you are not just creating a checklist; you are making an instruction set that any competent system can follow. This might take the form of a decision tree, a step-by-step SOP, or an AI prompt that includes key variables and context. Whatever the format, the intention is the same, preserve judgment without needing to repeat it.

Think about how much of your day is spent clarifying things you've already explained. Responding to slightly different versions of the same question. Tweaking a template that should have been dynamic. Re-explaining your process to someone who wasn't present the first time. Each of these interactions is a moment where the machine could have been taught to respond, redirect, or resolve without your intervention.

One of the most potent aspects of teaching the machine is its compounding nature. Every insight you embed becomes permanent infrastructure. When a client asks a nuanced question, and you take the time to build that answer into your onboarding sequence, that knowledge becomes evergreen. When you write a dynamic response into your AI chat tool, that intelligence scales infinitely. You're not just answering a question, you're preventing it from needing to be asked again.

But teaching the machine isn't just about writing better instructions. It's about encoding context. This is where most systems break down, not in the task execution, but in the interpretation. Machines don't do nuance unless you teach them.

That's why it's not enough to say what to do. You must say when, why, and under what conditions. This is the difference between a rule and a protocol. Rules follow. Protocols think.

For example, telling a system "send follow-up emails after three days" is a rule. Teaching it to wait longer if the client has already replied, or to escalate if there's urgency in the language, is protocol. These protocols come from paying attention to the patterns that exist just under the surface of your day-to-day decisions, the little if-this-then-that logic gates you've been executing silently for years. Once you start surfacing them, the machine can begin to operate not just with speed, but with judgment.

Another overlooked dimension of this work is iteration. Machines don't improve unless you train them to. Just because something works once doesn't mean it's optimized. The best operators constantly review system outputs, not to intervene, but to refine. They look for where the machine fell short, where the prompt misunderstood the context, where the automation skipped a step, or triggered too broadly. These are not failures. They are feedback loops. Every refinement makes the system stronger.

The most elegant systems are not the ones that require the most horsepower. They are the ones that embed the most apparent logic. A simple decision tree can outperform an expensive AI model if it's rooted in deep domain knowledge. That's why teaching the machine is a human act; it is about extracting insight, not just input. It requires reflection. What am I doing when I make this decision? What signals am I watching for?

What red flags change my course? When you externalize these reflections, you are creating leverage that operates independently of your presence.

This doesn't mean removing all human judgment. It means reserving it for where it matters most. Machines don't replace wisdom; they absorb repetition. They hold the routine, so your mind can roam. They take care of the 80% that can be predicted, so you can focus on the 20% that still surprises you.

There's also an emotional benefit here. When systems do the remembering for you, your cognitive load drops. You're not holding a hundred decisions in your head. You're not worried about forgetting to follow up, adjust a setting, or re-communicate a policy. You've taught the machine to think like you, act like you, and scale like you. You become more present because you are less preoccupied.

In team environments, teaching the machine has a cultural effect. It decentralizes competence. No one hoards knowledge because the system shares it. Onboarding becomes a process of accessing intelligence, not decoding hierarchy. Performance becomes more about interaction with the system than proximity to the founder. You've created a business where excellence is baked in, not handed down.

But perhaps the most liberating part of teaching the machine is that it redefines what it means to grow. You are no longer scaling by adding bodies. You're scaling by replicating intelligence. This is more than efficiency; it's sustainability. You are building something that gets better with each use. Something that learns every time you do. Something that doesn't need to be reminded, re-taught, or reinterpreted. Something that, over time, becomes an extension of your thinking at its best.

In the end, the machine is not magical. It is obedient. It will do what you teach it, no more and no less. The real magic is in your clarity, your ability to observe yourself, distill your decisions, and encode your edge. When you do this well, every system becomes a student. And every student becomes a source of scale.

Because in the world of artificial leverage, your job is not just to build. The goal is to teach your creation to operate independently. That's when freedom begins.

Chapter 40, Leverage as Legacy

Why building intelligently now pays dividends for years.

Most people think about legacy as something you leave behind, such as a memoir, a business, or a charitable foundation. But in the world of artificial leverage, legacy takes on a different texture. It's not merely what endures after you're gone. It's what continues to produce, adapt, and evolve without your ongoing effort. It is infrastructure that outlives your attention. Intelligence that scales without your supervision. Leverage that doesn't expire with your availability.

To build a legacy through leverage is to make a commitment to intentional systems thinking. It's the refusal to build for the moment when you could create for the decade. It's the decision to codify insight instead of hoarding it. To engineer tools that compound value even after you've walked away from the dashboard. This is not about immortality. It's about dignity. The dignity of knowing that the best of your work didn't die inside your inbox or behind a login screen.

Leverage becomes a legacy when it removes you as the bottleneck while retaining your perspective. That is a subtle but critical distinction. You are not cloning yourself. You are curating what deserves to persist. You are extracting your values, your standards, and your hard-won lessons into processes that carry forward even when you're no longer available to defend or explain them. Legacy, then, is not about presence. It's about imprint.

To get there, you must begin asking different questions. Not just "What needs to get done?" but "What do I want to be true five years from now, without me having to redo this work?" That question recalibrates your standards. You no longer settle for the quick fix or the brittle workaround. You start designing for a duration. For adaptability. For a utility that extends beyond the current quarter. You start building with the understanding that sound systems age well, and great systems become teaching tools for the next generation.

Please think of how we remember confident thinkers, creators, or builders. It's rarely just their output. It's the clarity of the systems they created, the philosophies, frameworks, and practices that others could adopt, adapt, and extend. These people didn't just perform well. They encoded their performance. They left instructions, even if unspoken, about how to navigate complexity with elegance. That is leverage at its most refined, wisdom made operational.

This kind of legacy doesn't require fame. It requires clarity. The small business owner who turns their approach to customer experience into a documented, repeatable workflow is engaging in legacy work. The designer who creates a scalable design system that others can build on is doing legacy work. The educator who writes modular curricula that other teachers can remix is investing in legacy. The entrepreneur who documents decision logic so that others can lead with confidence is creating a legacy in action.

The tragedy is that most people don't recognize legacy opportunities while they're happening. They're too busy reacting.

Too caught up in solving today's version of the problem to build the system that solves tomorrow's variations of it. They rewrite the same email dozens of times. They rebuild the same dashboard every launch cycle. They hire and rehire without ever creating the structure that eliminates the guesswork. What could have been a repeatable edge becomes a repeating burden.

Legacy through leverage is the antidote. It requires a moment of pause. A decision to step back, observe the patterns, and encode the lessons. It's not glamorous. It often doesn't feel urgent. But it's the work that makes all future work lighter. It's the force multiplier that you only truly appreciate when you see someone else succeed using what you built, not because they copied you, but because your system gave them a head start.

This approach also reframes your relationship with change. When systems are built for legacy, they are designed to flex, not fracture. They include feedback loops. They make room for updates. They aren't fragile monuments. They are living organisms that absorb insight, refine behavior, and expand capacity. That's what separates brittle leverage from durable leverage—the former cracks under evolution. The latter evolves by design.

And what about the emotional side of legacy? Many builders struggle to let go because they believe that release equals irrelevance. But the opposite is true. The more transferable your knowledge, the more influential you become. Influence is not control. It is continuity. When your judgment becomes part of the system, you no longer need to be present to make a difference.

You've made yourself unnecessary to the daily mechanics but indispensable to the architecture.

This is where we return to the idea of sovereignty. True legacy doesn't just benefit others; it liberates you. It gives you optionality without loss of contribution. You don't have to be in every meeting, every document, every decision. And yet, the work continues. The value spreads. The ideas evolve. And you're free to move upstream, into deeper thinking, broader contexts, or even entirely new pursuits.

For some, this leads to mentorship. For others, it means building multiple ventures with the same foundational patterns. For many, it simply allows for rest because rest becomes possible not when you slow down, but when you've built something that keeps going, without needing you to push it.

What makes this all possible is that artificial leverage is not just technical. It is philosophical. You're not just automating. You're capturing insight. You're not just delegating. You're instilling logic. You're not just scaling. You're preserving fidelity. And when you do it with care, the byproduct is a body of work that continues to serve long after the adrenaline wears off.

Legacy, then, is not the final chapter. It's the invisible thread. It's what turns effort into infrastructure. What turns attention into permanence. It's what allows your work to travel further than your reach. It's what makes systems humane, businesses resilient, and creativity regenerative.

And the most remarkable part? It begins today. Not with a grand gesture. Not with a retirement plan. But with a single decision to stop redoing what could have been designed once with clarity and care. With one afternoon spent documenting the why, not just the what. With a moment of stillness to say, this process, this insight, this asset, deserves to live on.

Because leverage is not about more, it's about better. And when done right, it becomes a legacy, not something you leave behind, but something you live through, again and again, in every system that works without you.

Epilogue

The Leverage Life

What it means to build a life that scales beyond effort

You don't wake up one day and suddenly feel leveraged. There is no dramatic moment where the world shifts and you realize you've ascended beyond toil. Leverage, when done right, arrives quietly. It builds in layers, accumulates in systems, and unfolds through design. One morning, you notice that the friction is gone. The noise has reduced. The questions answer themselves. And the game you were playing no longer requires the same kind of fuel.

This is what the leverage life feels like, not a sprint to an exit, but a steady expansion of your freedom. It's not about doing less. It's about needing less energy to create the same, or greater, impact. It's not about disconnection. It's about reorientation. The mechanics no longer consume your time. It's available for the work that requires originality, discernment, and leadership. The work that cannot be templated.

In many ways, this book has not been about tools or automations or even systems. It has been about sovereignty. The ability to choose what deserves your energy. The freedom to design a business, a workflow, a creative life that supports your thinking instead of interrupting it. Sovereignty is not the elimination of obligation. It's the elevation of intent. When your infrastructure does the heavy lifting, your calendar becomes a map of your actual priorities, not your firefighting schedule.

Living the leverage life means rejecting the productivity arms race. You are no longer measuring success by output volume or inbox velocity. You're not playing the game of inbox zero or project board gymnastics. You are measuring the sustainability of your performance. You are designing your days not around capacity, but around clarity. You are asking, over and over, what does this system free me to think about?

This shift is subtle but radical. It moves you from being a producer to being a builder of producers. From executing to orchestrating. From scaling your energy to scaling your intelligence. And that distinction is everything. Your energy is finite. Your intelligence, when captured, is not.

When you teach the machine, codify your principles, and document instead of repeating, you create an asset that performs with or without you. And from that place, you begin to see what else becomes possible. You can step away without losing momentum. You can explore new projects without abandoning the old. You can rest without guilt because rest is not withdrawal; it is a recalibration.

But leverage is not an endpoint. It is a discipline. It must be maintained. Systems decay if left alone. Automations require review. Delegation loses fidelity if not inspected. This is the paradox of leverage, while it reduces your labor, it increases your responsibility to design wisely. You are no longer just a doer. You are a systems steward. A curator of clarity. A protector of principles. The reward is exponential capacity, but the requirement is intentional upkeep.

That upkeep, however, is rarely oppressive. Most people who commit to leveraging life find that their quality of thought improves. Their nervous system slows down. Their ambition stops cannibalizing their well-being. They realize that the purpose of leverage was never speed. It was space. And in that space, creativity blooms. Strategic thinking returns. The big bets become visible again. Not because you finally cleared your to-do list, but because your infrastructure now filters out everything that doesn't matter.

The leverage life is not reserved for tech founders or digital creators. It's not just for coders or systems nerds. It's available to anyone willing to build a thoughtful relationship with their work. The local business owner who automates scheduling, the nonprofit leader who trains their onboarding bot to speak in their voice, the consultant who turns their insights into an evergreen library of explainers, all of them are practicing artificial leverage. All of them are buying back the future with today's clarity.

That's what leverage ultimately gives you, time that compounds. Not time saved in minutes, but time reclaimed in direction. Time that moves with you, that echoes your thinking, which doesn't forget what you've already learned. The time that stops punishing you for your past ambition. Time that opens the door to what you thought you'd never have enough of, margin, calm, choice.

In a world that celebrates the hustle, the leverage life is a rebellion of design. It says, I will work hard, but I will not do it unthinkingly. I will build with care, not chaos. I will honor my attention by protecting it. I will leave behind not just content, clients, or campaigns, but clarity. I will build systems that are kind to my future self.

And when others ask how you manage it all, how you create so consistently, how you make it look effortless, you'll know the truth. It's not that you're superhuman. It's that your systems are finally working as hard as you do. And maybe harder.

This is the reward of artificial leverage. Not just the productivity. Not just the profit. But the peace that comes from knowing you've built something that lasts. Something that doesn't just scale. Something that sustains.

Because in the end, the most valuable asset is not the tool, the tactic, or the stack. You can build a life that reflects your values, protects your energy, and amplifies your genius, without burning you out in the process.

That is the leverage of life. Quiet. Durable. Free.

Other Books by David Webb

The Book On Life Unscripted
The Book On Risk Management in Payments
The Book On Strategic Obsession
The Book On High-Stakes Thinking

About The Author

David Webb is a seasoned entrepreneur and business leader with more than three decades of experience at the intersection of technology, finance, and services. As the founder and CEO of multiple ventures—some celebrated successes and some hard-learned failures—he has cultivated a reputation for turning complexity into clarity, driving growth, and leading organizations through periods of both turbulence and transformation. His career has been defined by a willingness to take calculated risks, embrace innovation, and pursue opportunities others often overlook.

David's debut book, Life Unscripted, What You Should Have Learned in High School, distilled years of professional and personal experience into a practical guide for navigating the overlooked realities of adulthood. His second, The Book On Risk Management in Payments, marked a decisive step into specialized territory, tackling one of the most pressing challenges in global commerce, how to anticipate threats, safeguard trust, and manage risk in a world where money moves faster than regulation.

With his third book, The Book On Strategic Obsession, How to Turn Long-Term Thinking Into a Competitive Weapon, David advanced his mission further by exploring the discipline of sustained, long-horizon thinking as a defining advantage in leadership and strategy. Drawing from decades at the intersection of leadership, risk, and relentless execution, he reframed strategy not as a static plan on paper, but as an enduring obsession that separates fleeting achievements from lasting success.

His fourth book, The Book On High-Stakes Thinking, How to Make Decisions That Actually Matter, pushed into even more urgent terrain—the art of thinking clearly when the consequences are severe. Here, David dissected how individuals and organizations can cultivate mental frameworks that withstand pressure, avoid cognitive traps, and transform decisive moments into defining victories.

His fifth book, The Book On Artificial Leverage, How to Use Tools, Technology, and Systems to Outwork Entire Teams Without Burnout, reflects David's conviction that the future of performance will belong not to those who grind the hardest, but to those who design intelligently. In this work, he explores how entrepreneurs, professionals, and creators can harness automation, AI, and systems-thinking to achieve outsized impact without sacrificing sustainability. Where his earlier works examined risk, strategy, and high-stakes decision-making, Artificial Leverage completes the progression by showing how to build enduring capacity in a world where human effort alone is no longer enough.

Beyond writing and business, David remains committed to mentoring entrepreneurs and contributing to community initiatives that promote education, resilience, and personal growth. Whether in boardrooms, classrooms, or in print, his work reflects a consistent theme, empowering others to think critically, act decisively, and build systems that endure.

About The Publisher

Welcome to The Book On Publishing

At The Book On Publishing, we believe in rewriting the rules of learning. Whether you're chasing your next big idea, building a better life, or simply curious about what should have been taught in school, you've come to the right place.

We're a platform built for dreamers, doers, and lifelong learners, offering bold, practical books and tools that empower you to take charge of your journey. From real-world skills to mindset mastery, we publish the book on what matters.

No fluff. No lectures. Just what you need to know, delivered with clarity, purpose, and a spark of curiosity.

Start exploring. Start growing. Start writing your story.

Read more at https,//thebookon.ca.

DAVID WEBB

Acknowledgment of AI Assistance

Portions of this book were developed with the support of AI. While every word has been carefully reviewed and refined by the author, AI served as a valuable tool for brainstorming, editing, and structuring ideas. Its assistance helped accelerate the creative process and bring clarity to complex topics.

www.ingramcontent.com/pod-product-compliance
Lightning Source LLC
Chambersburg PA
CBHW071723120626
46550CB00001B/358